Dot to Dot Book For Kids Ages 8-12

This book belongs to:

_____

This book is filled with 100 amazing connect the dots activities!
The activities are separated into 3 levels; ranging from easy to challenging!

The book features:

- 100 FUN DOT TO DOT ACTIVITIES
- COLOR-IN IMAGES AFTER COMPLETION
- LARGE SIZE PAGES
- 3 PROGRESSIVE LEVELS
- COMPLETION CERTIFICATE AT THE END

For the Parent

Dot to dot puzzles help your child to learn how to count numbers and develop fine motor skills by tracing the lines. Continued practice improves hand-eye coordination and helps to improve your kid's dexterity and muscle memory through drawing a line and following the dots to complete the image.
Dot to dot activities also helps to nurture the development of our child's brain and improves visualization skills, thought processes, problem solving skills and emotional intelligence.

Level 1

Let's start! In this level, you will have to connect the dots in each activity.

Ready? Let's go!

3

4

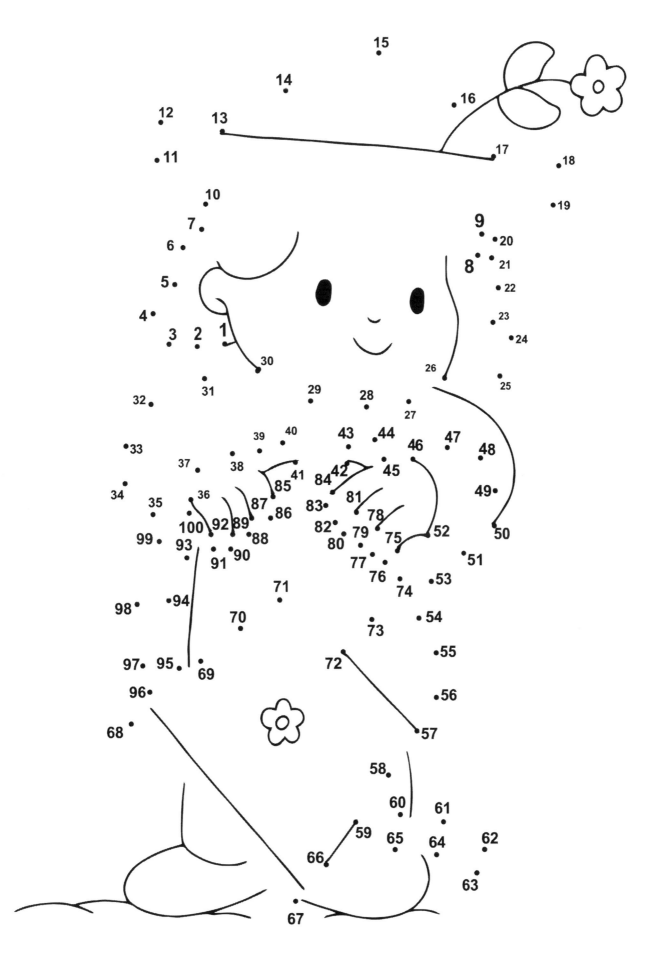

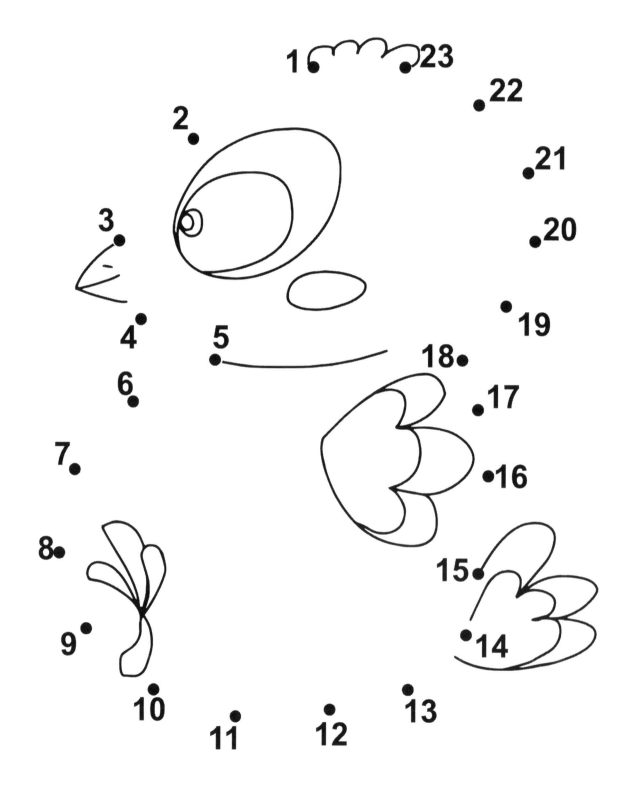

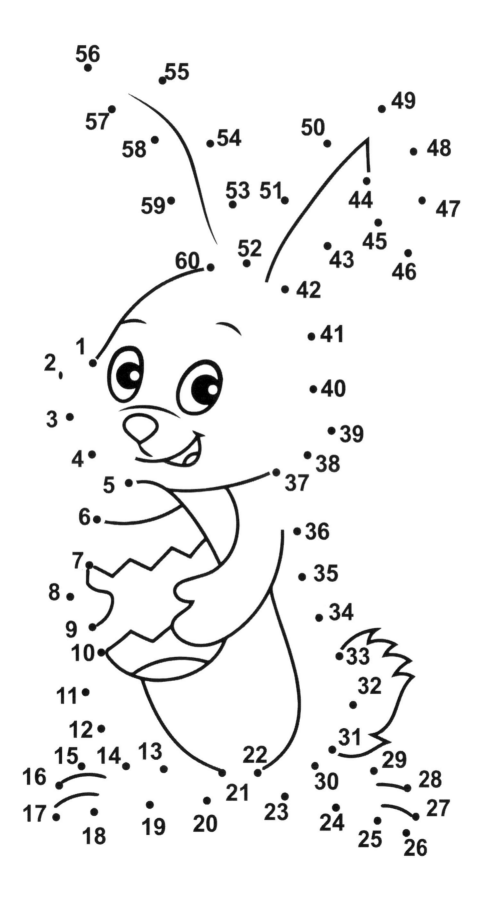

8

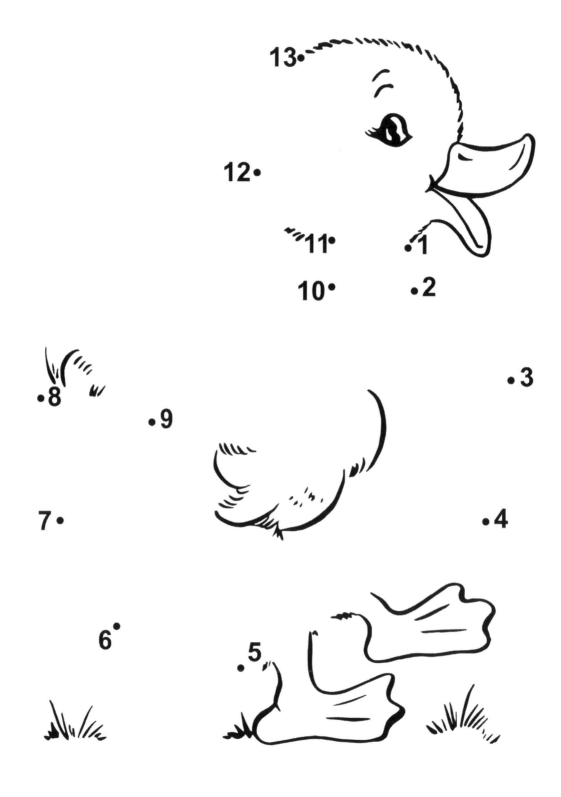

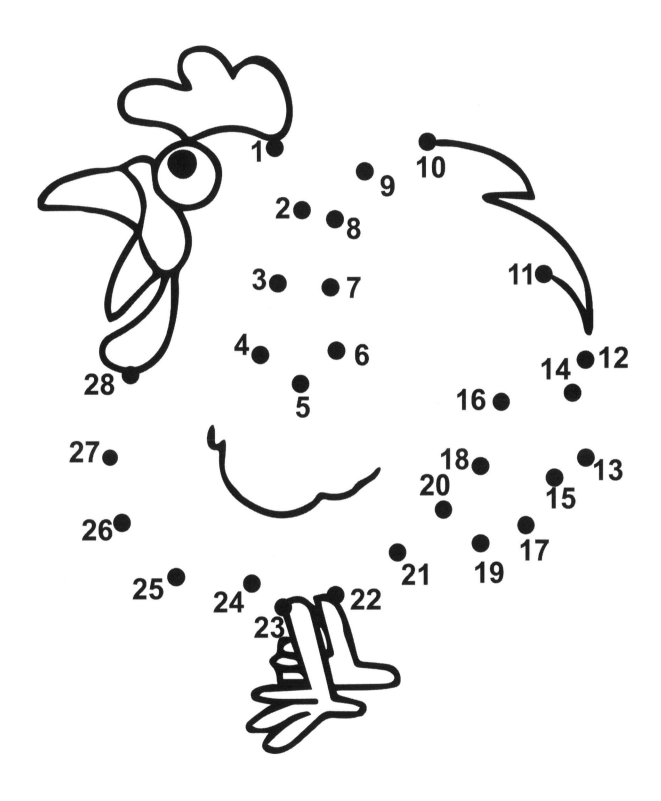

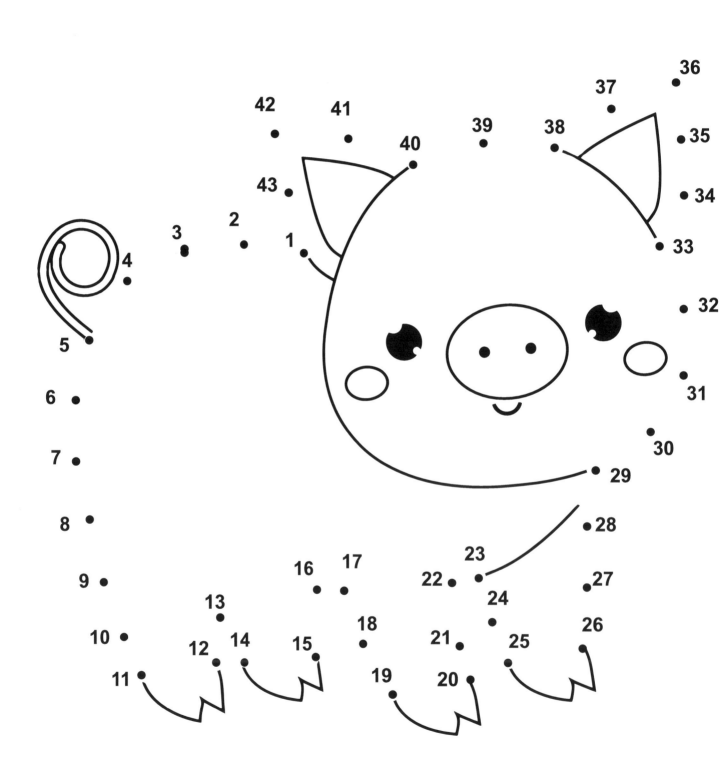

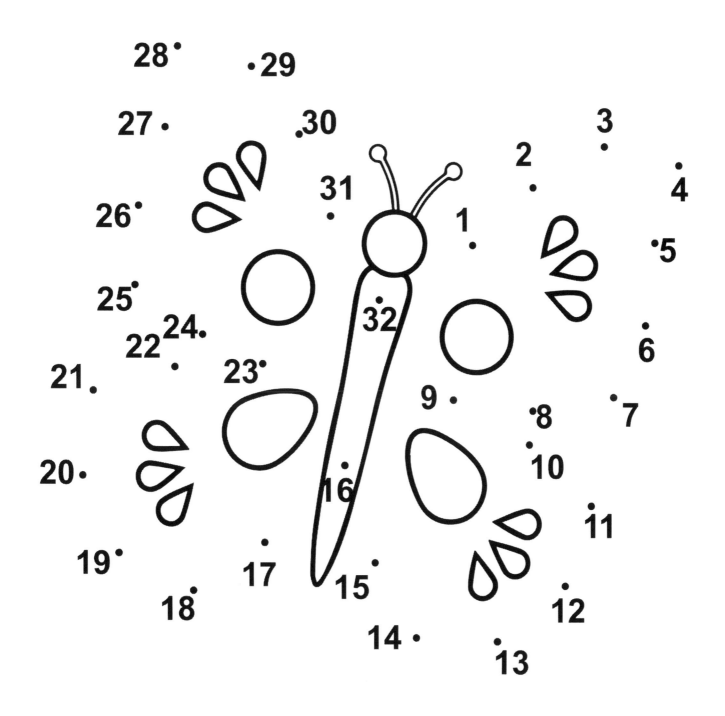

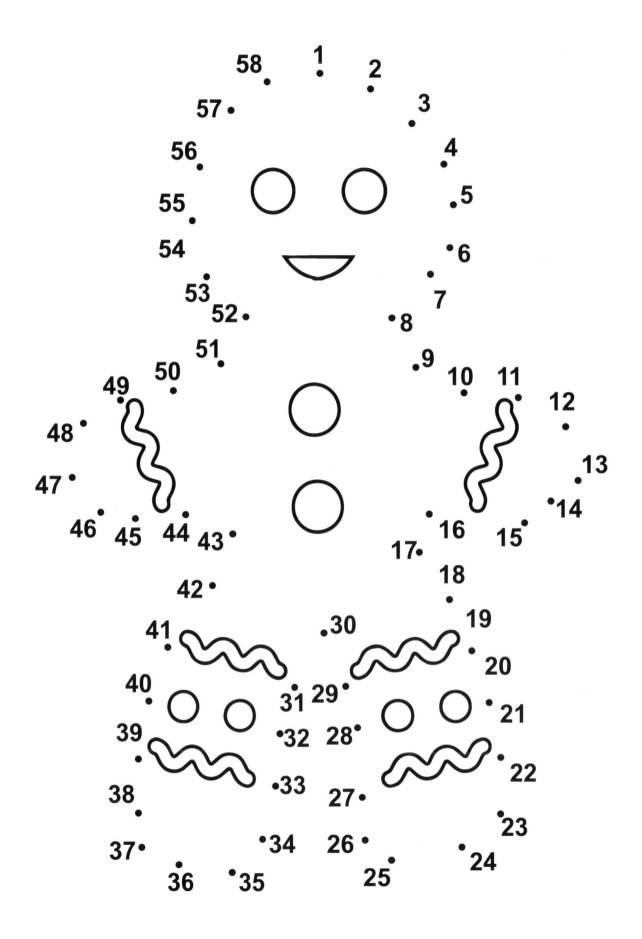

13

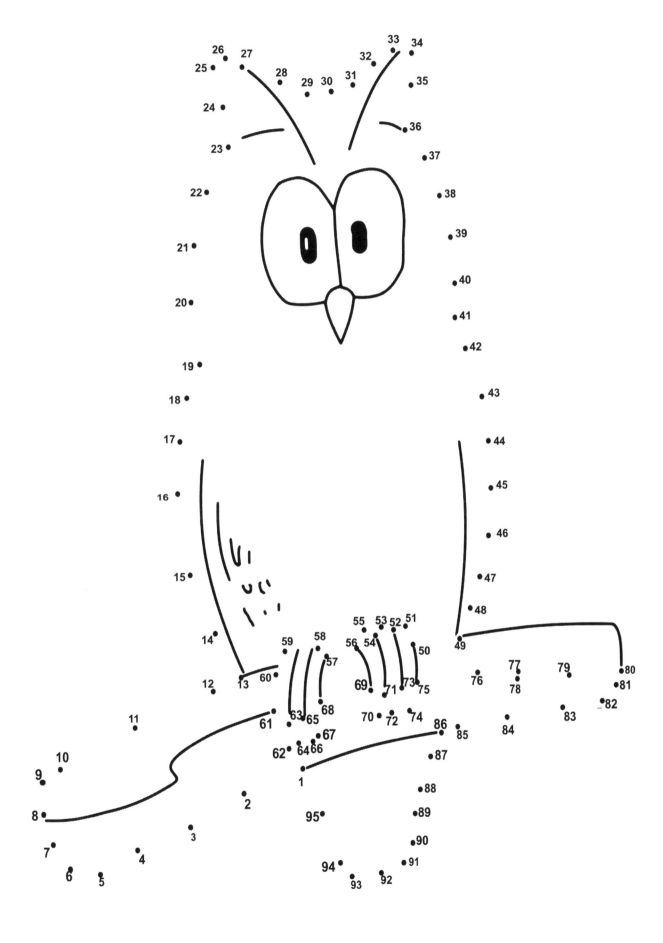

14

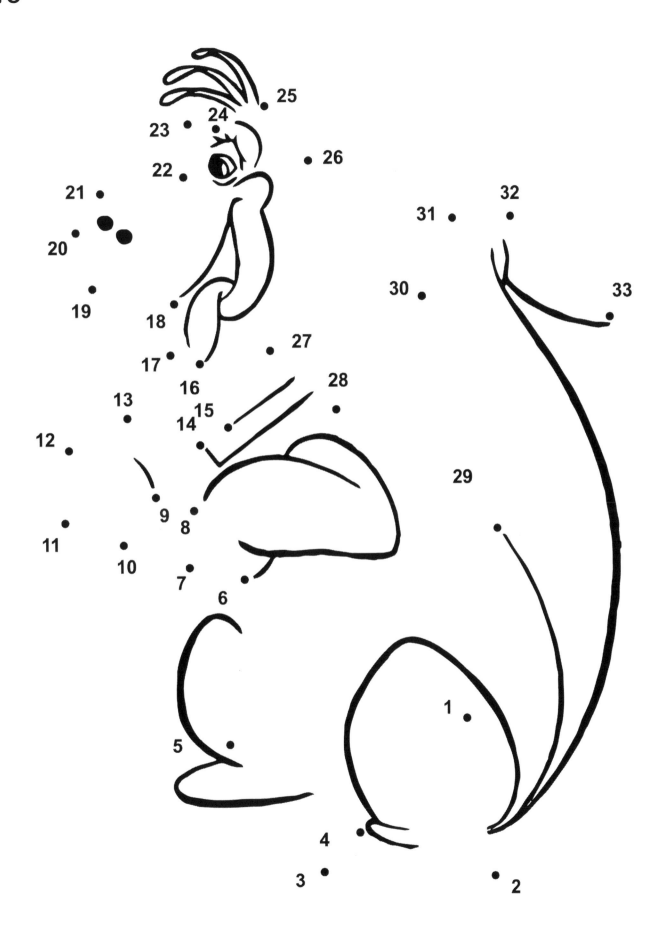

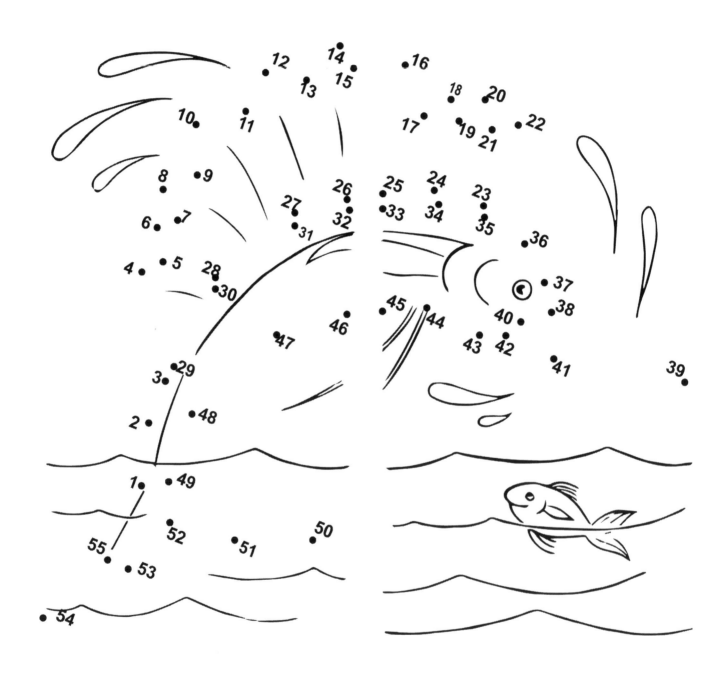

17

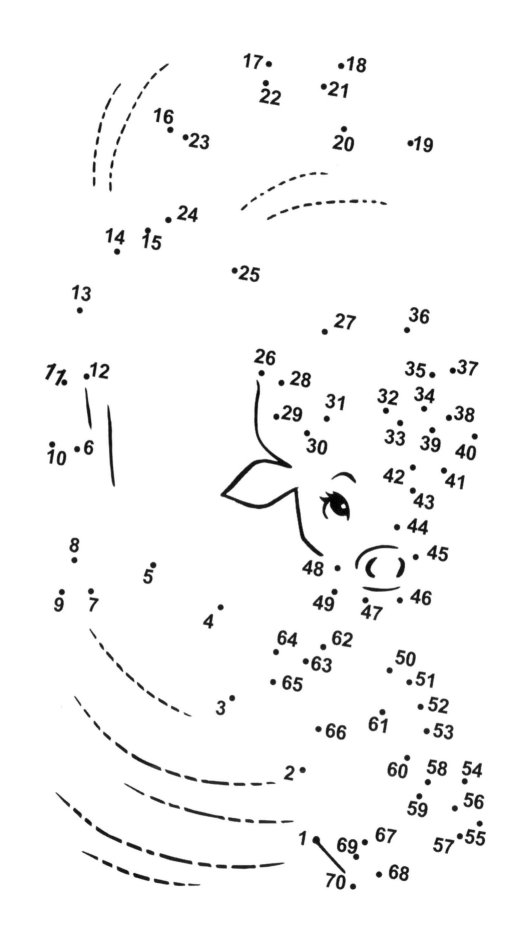

19

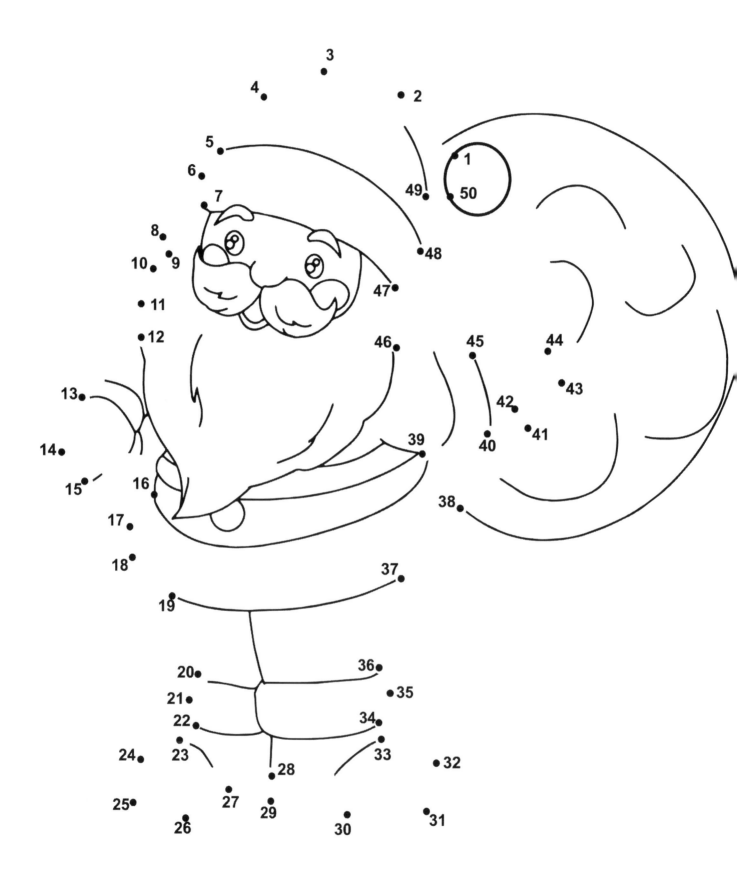

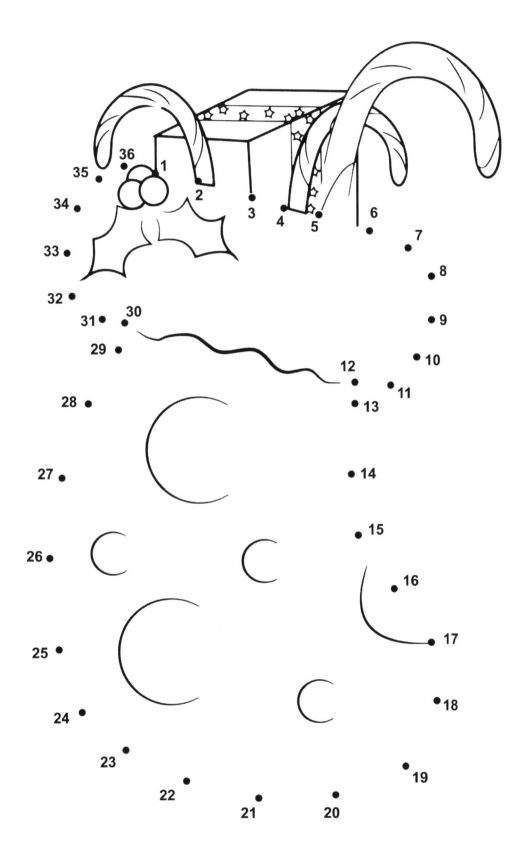

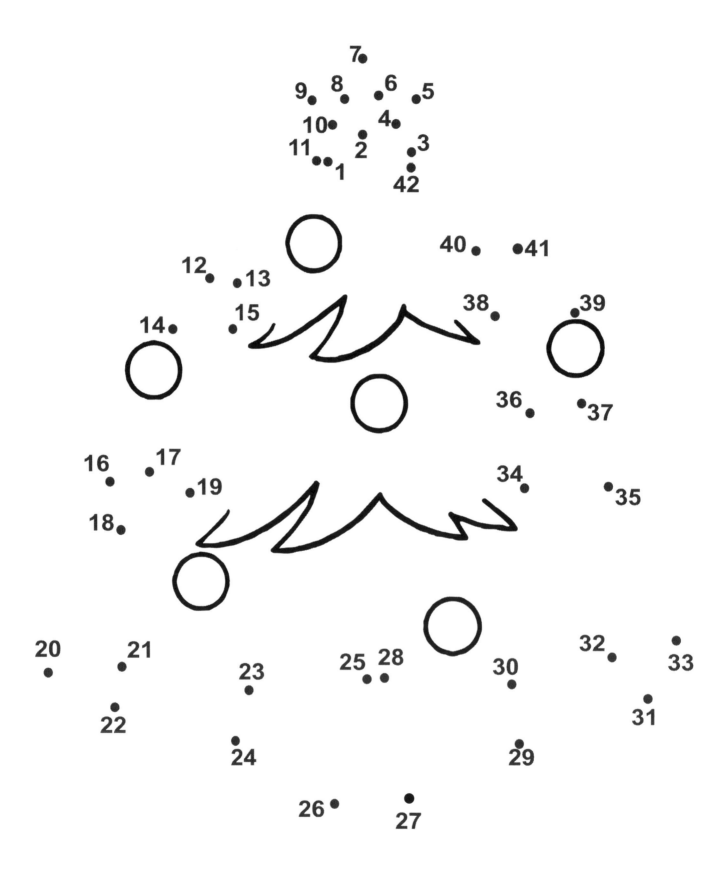

23

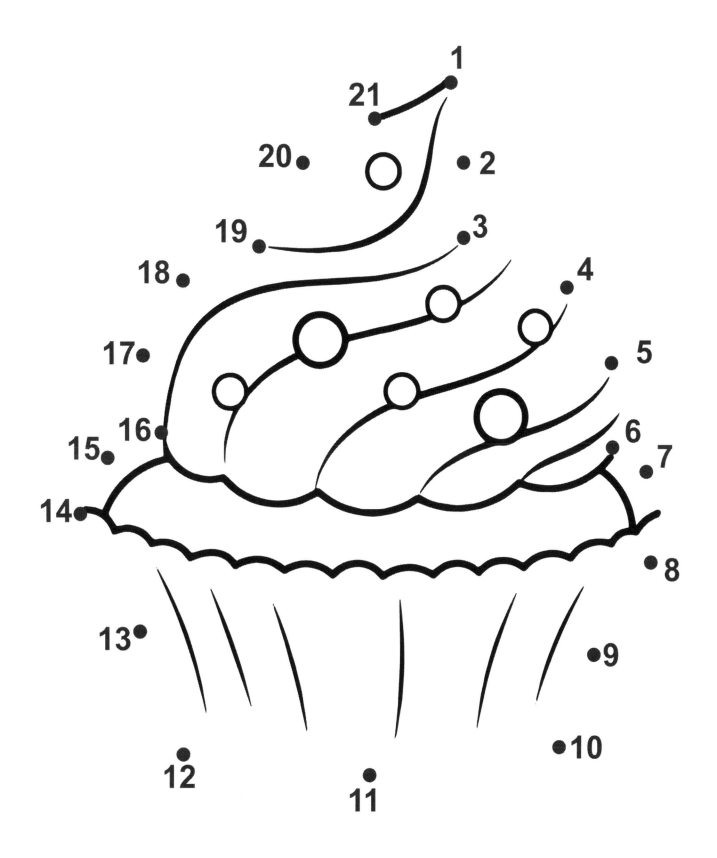

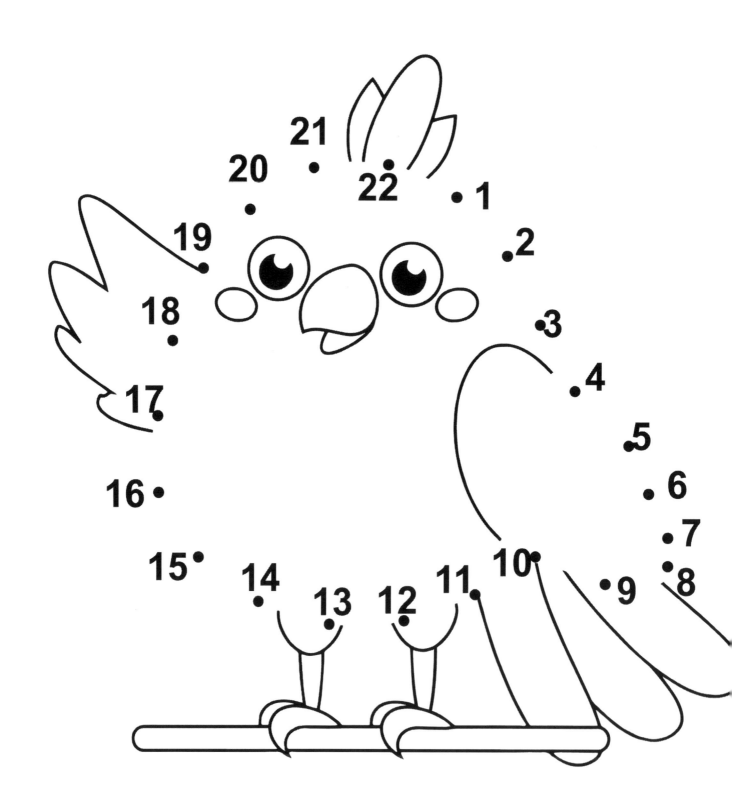

25

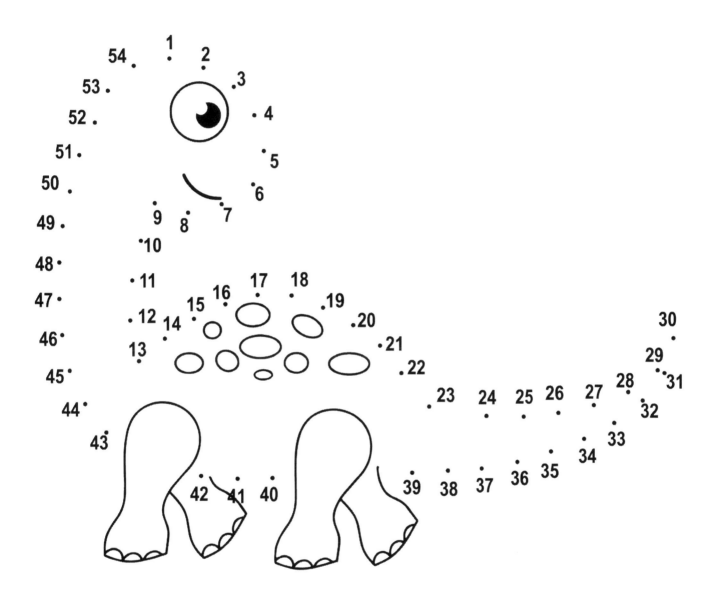

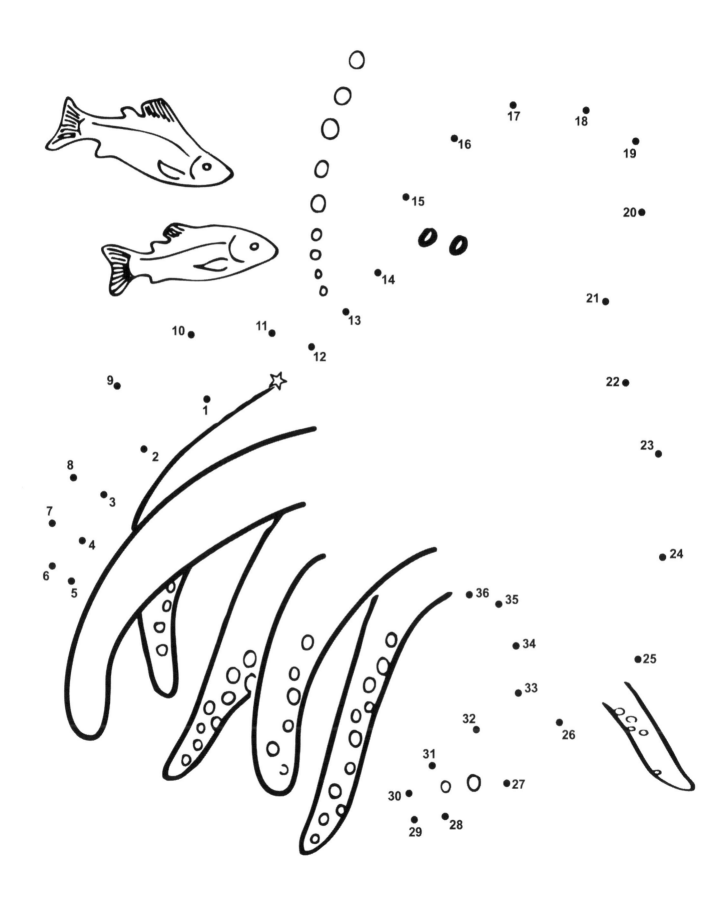

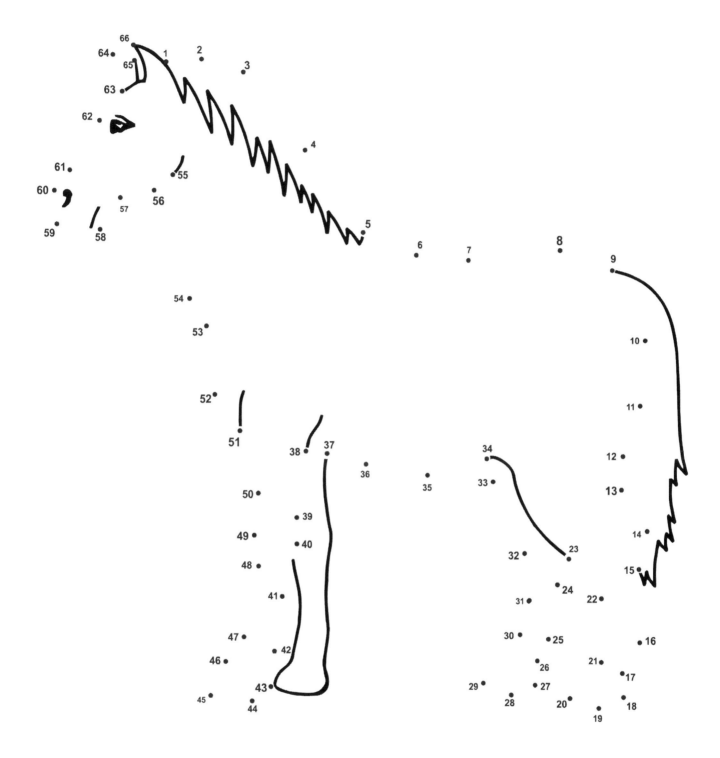

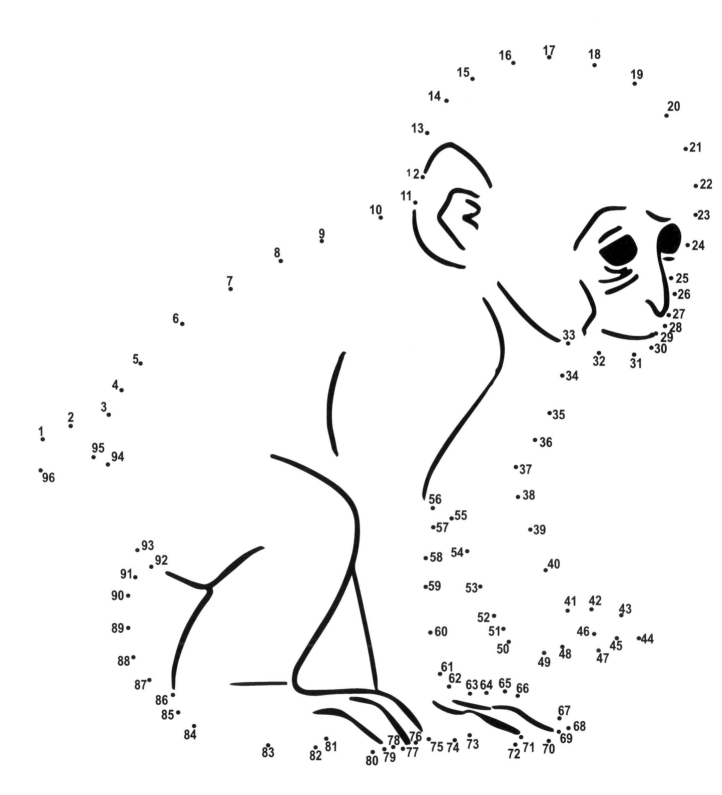

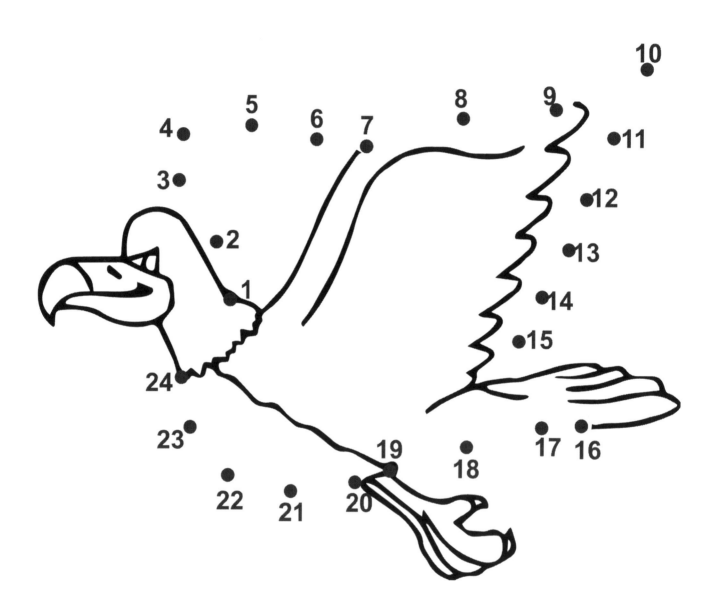

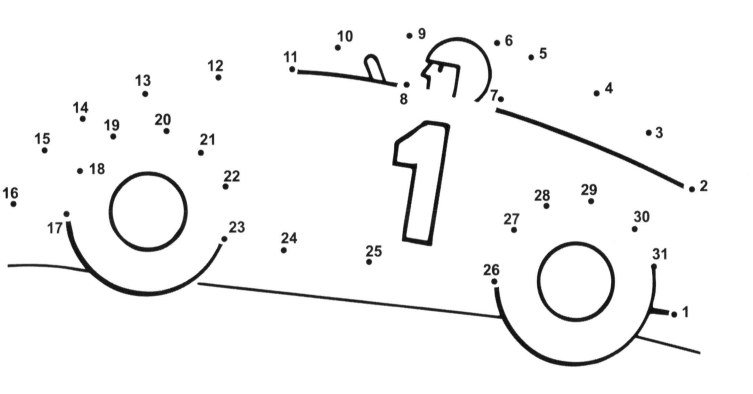

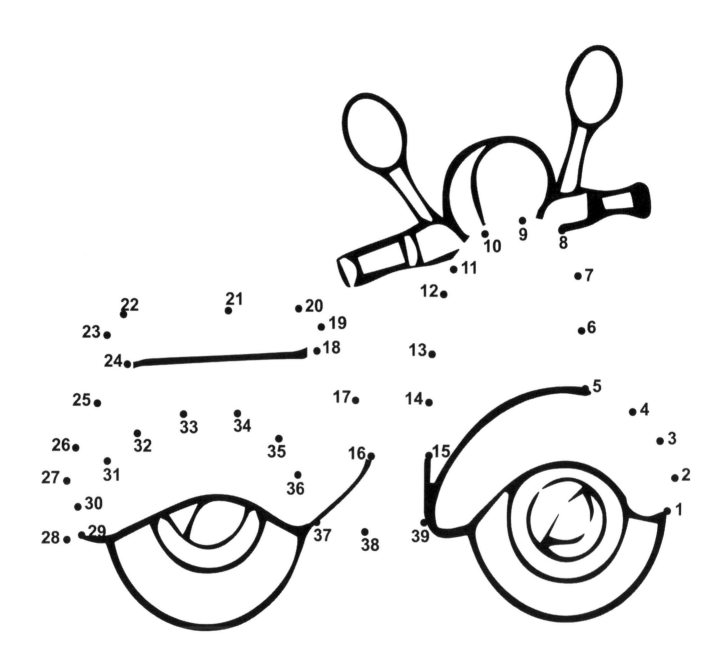

Level 2

In this level, you will have connect 10 + dots.

Ready? Let's go!

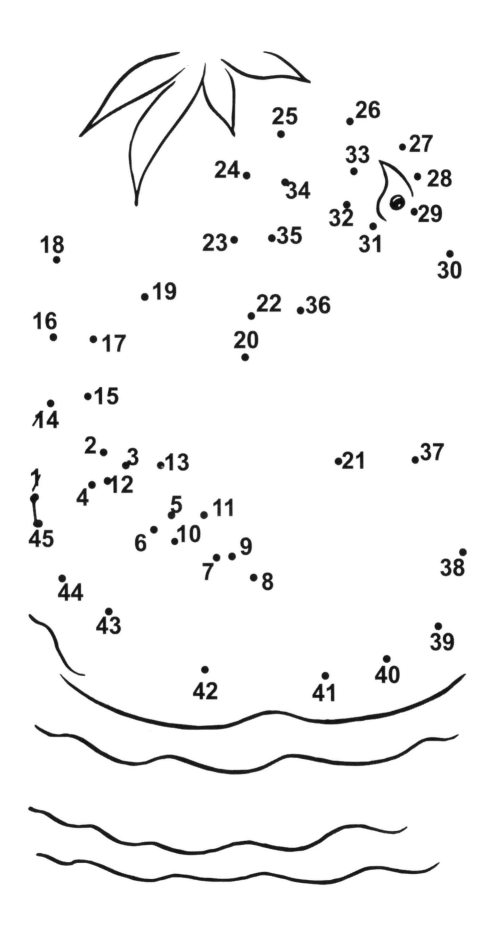

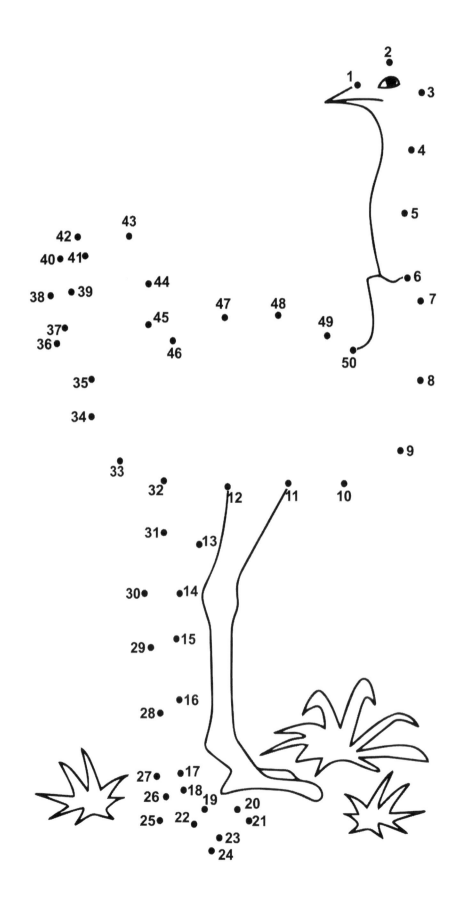

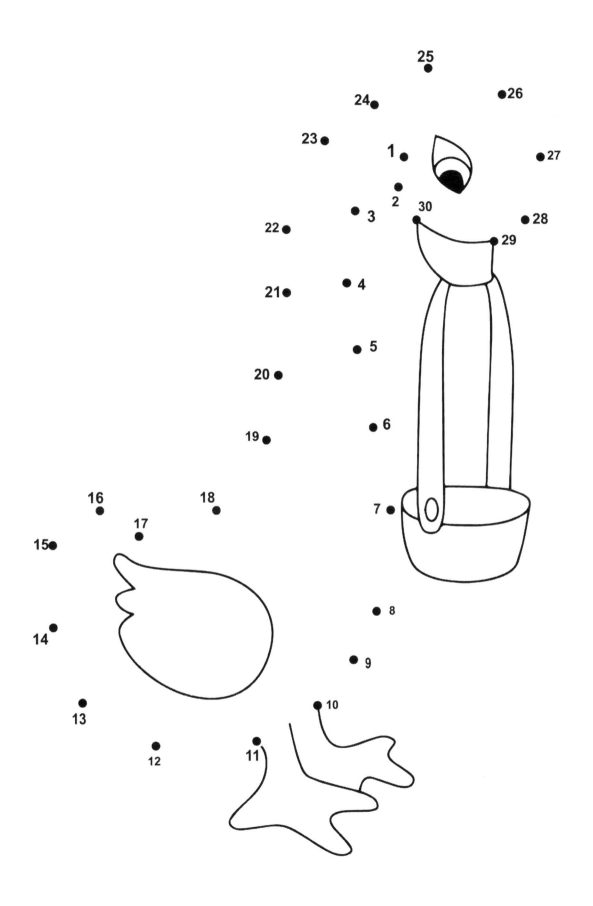

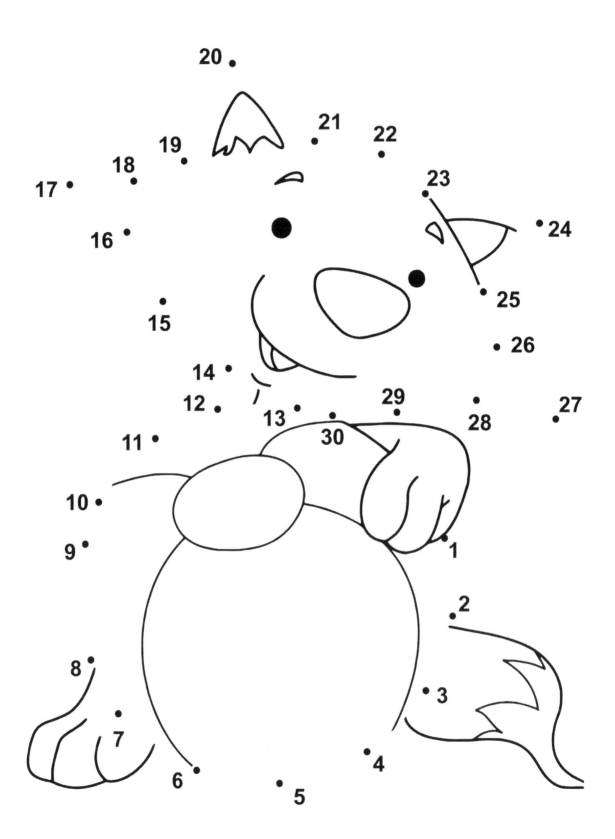

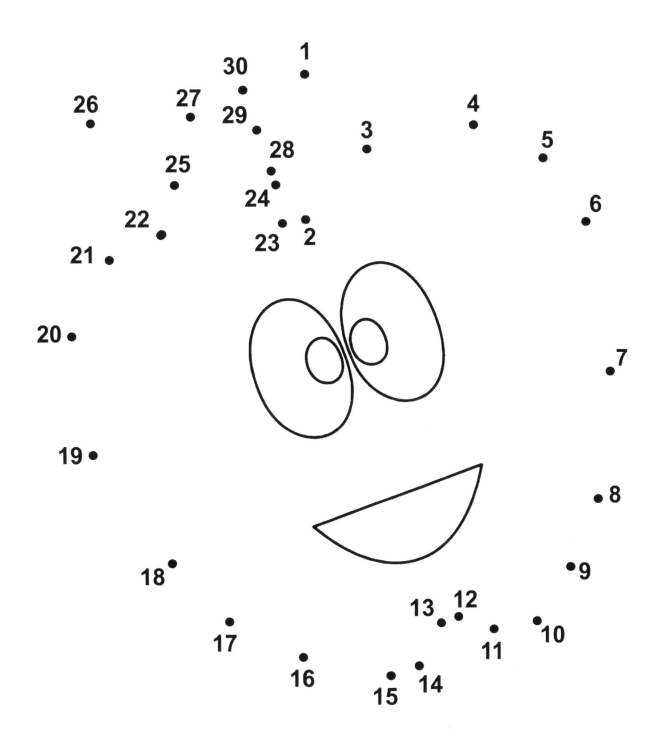

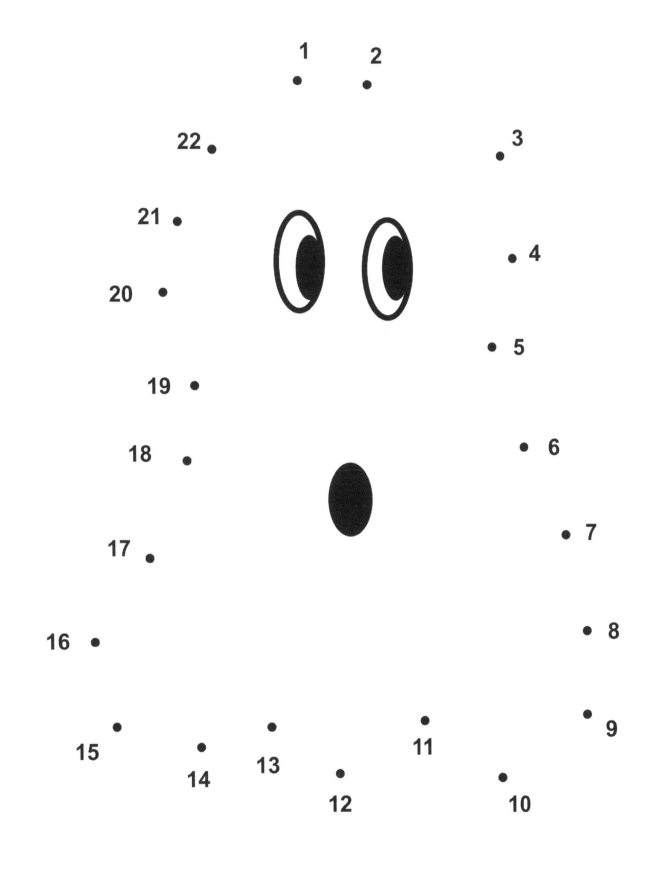

42

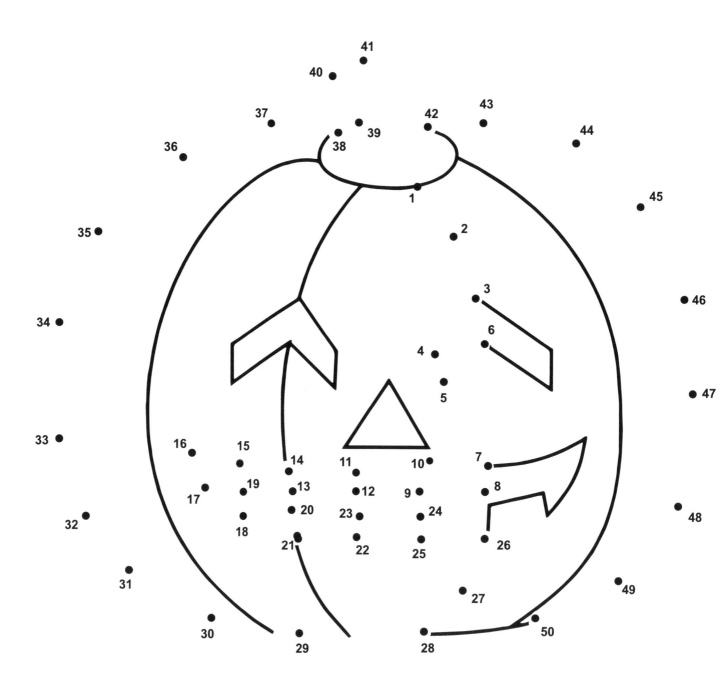

43

19

18

7

8

16 •   **13**
            •

• **10**

15   **14**   **12**   **11**

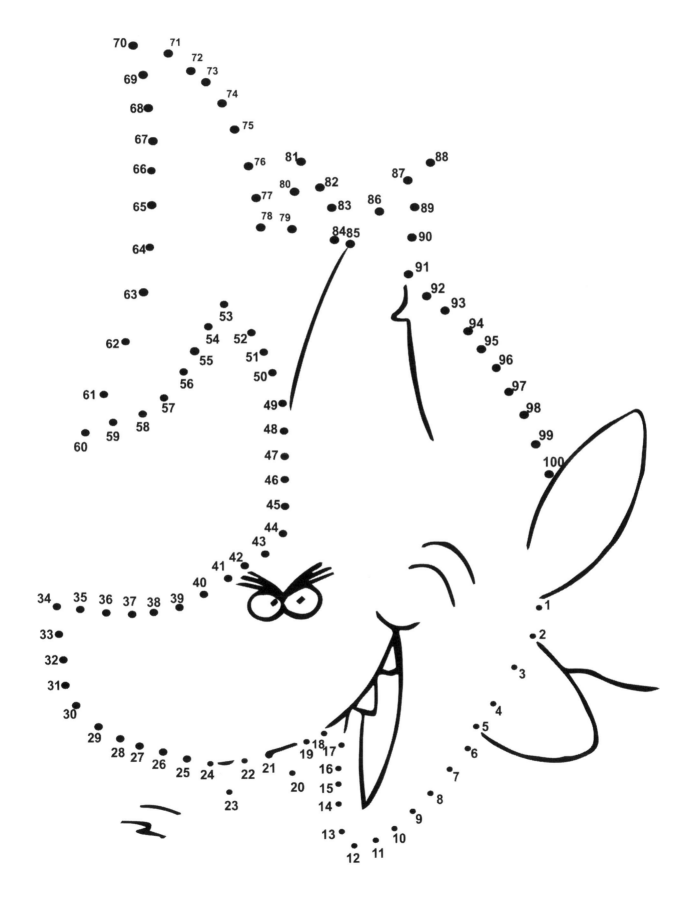

47

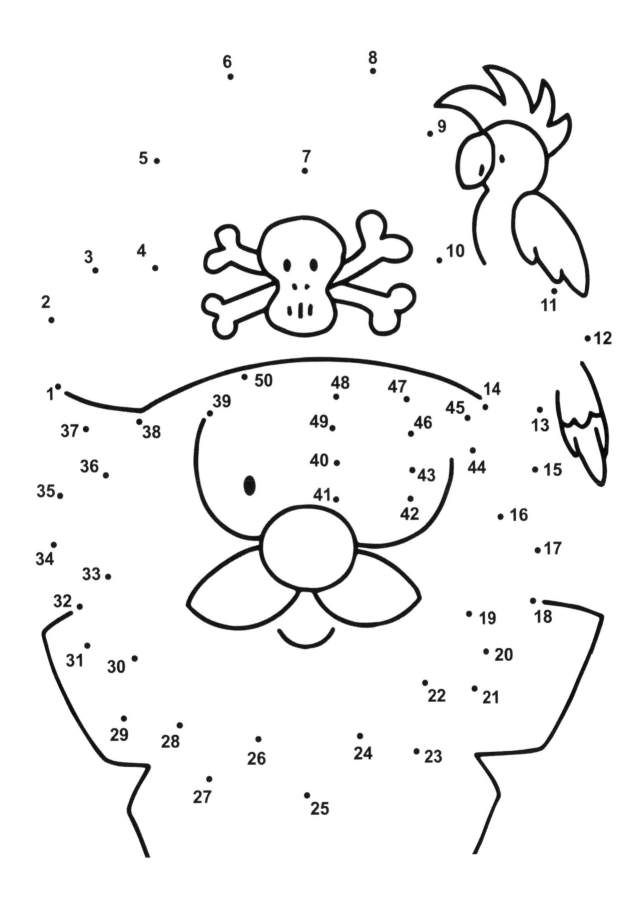

50

51

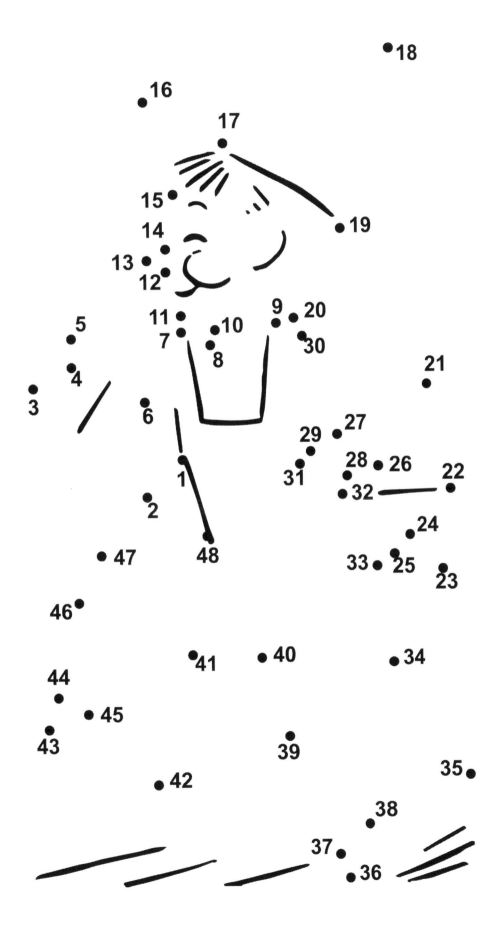

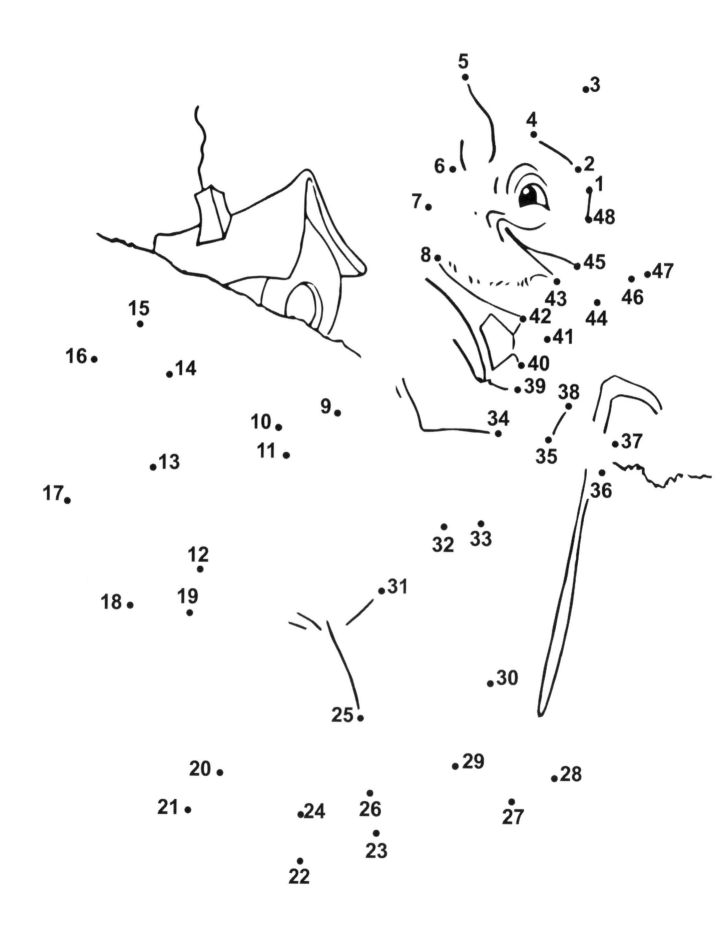

53

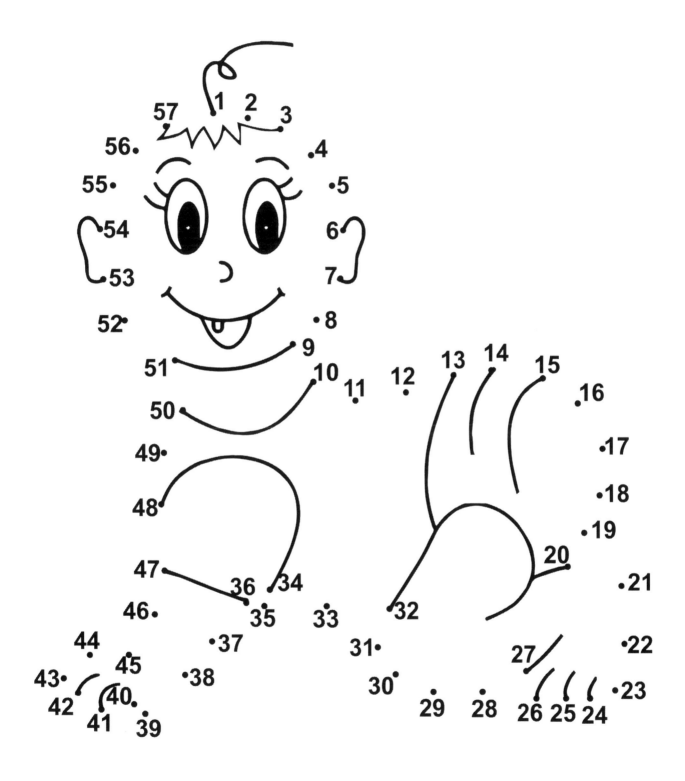

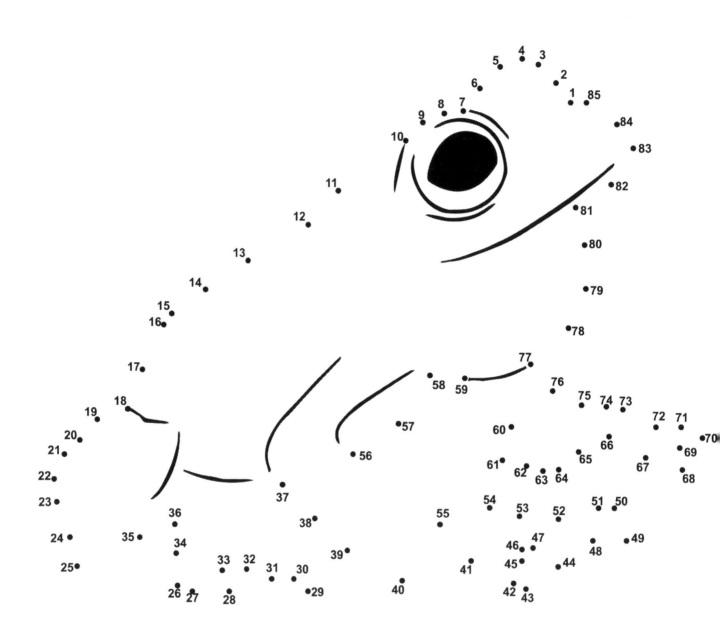

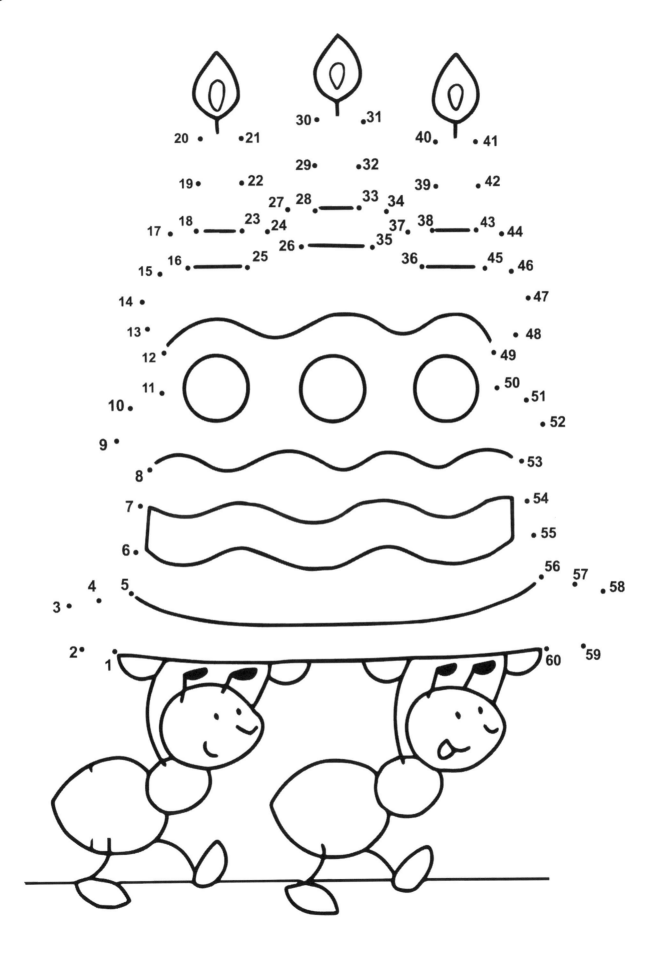

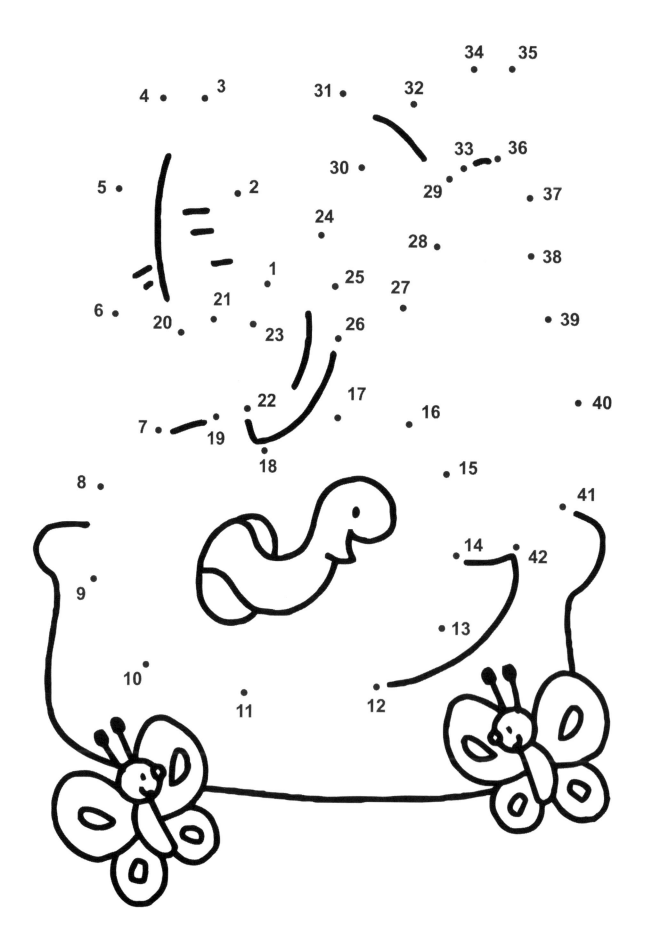

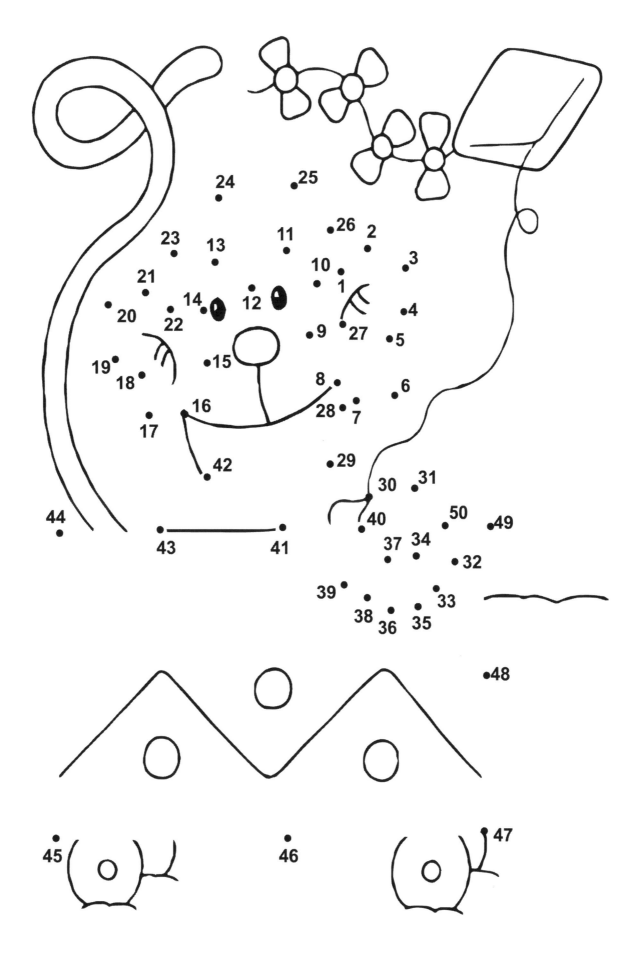

58

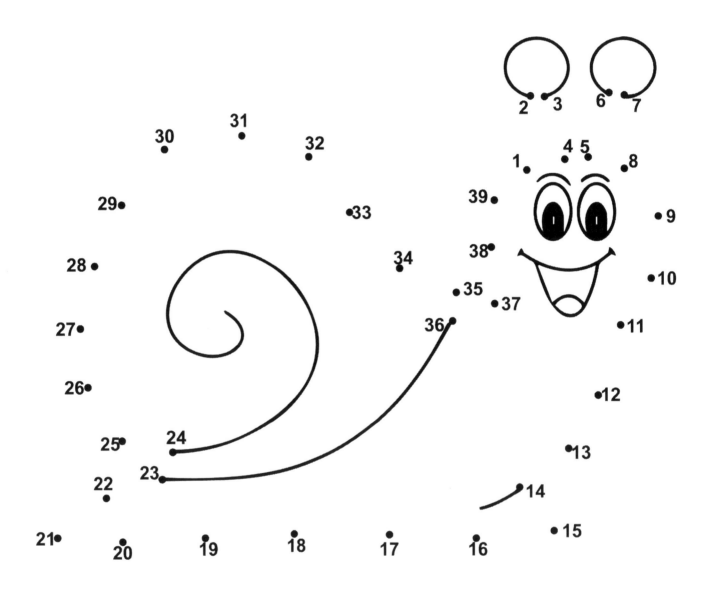

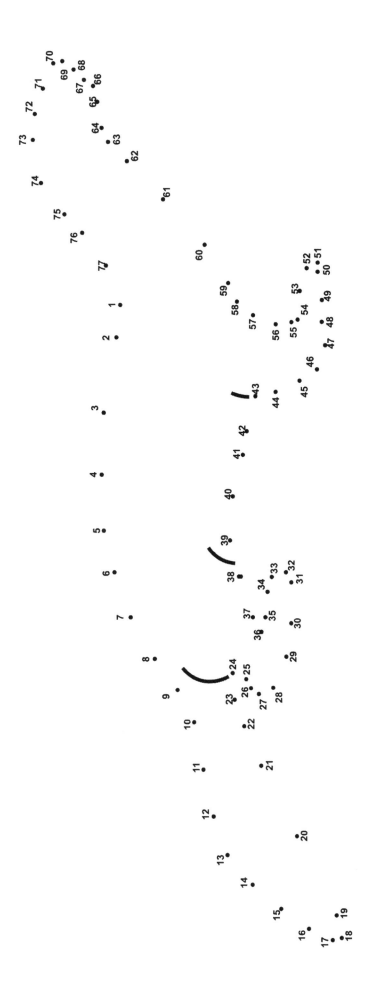

60

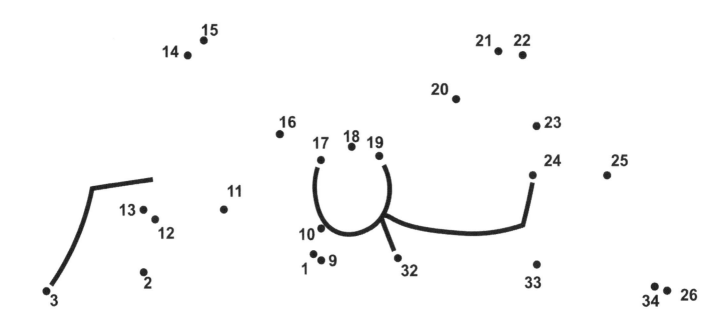

61

62

63

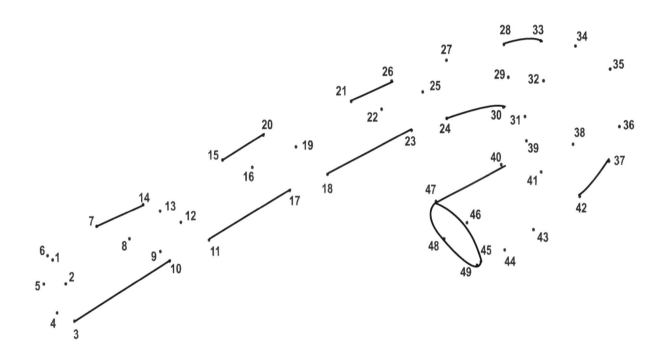

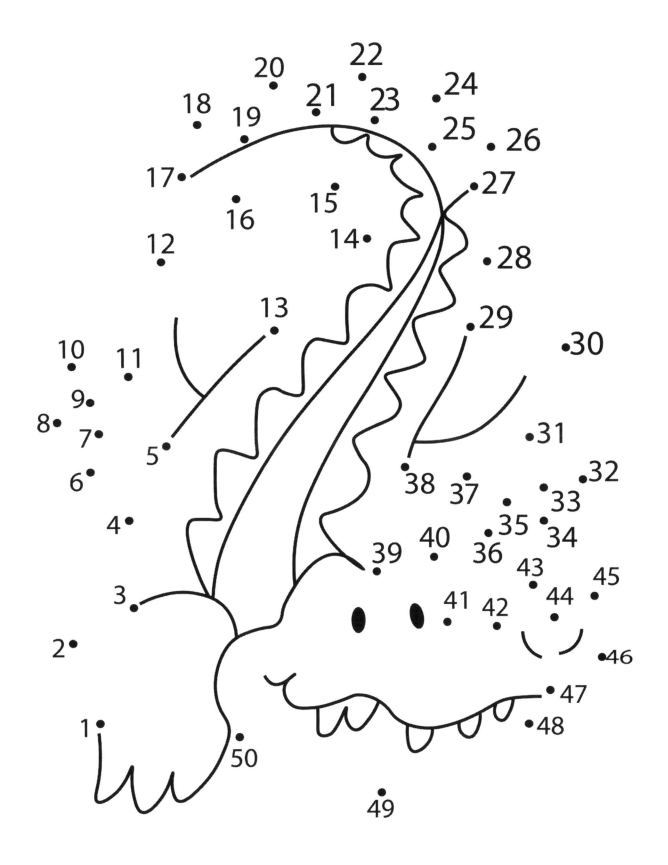

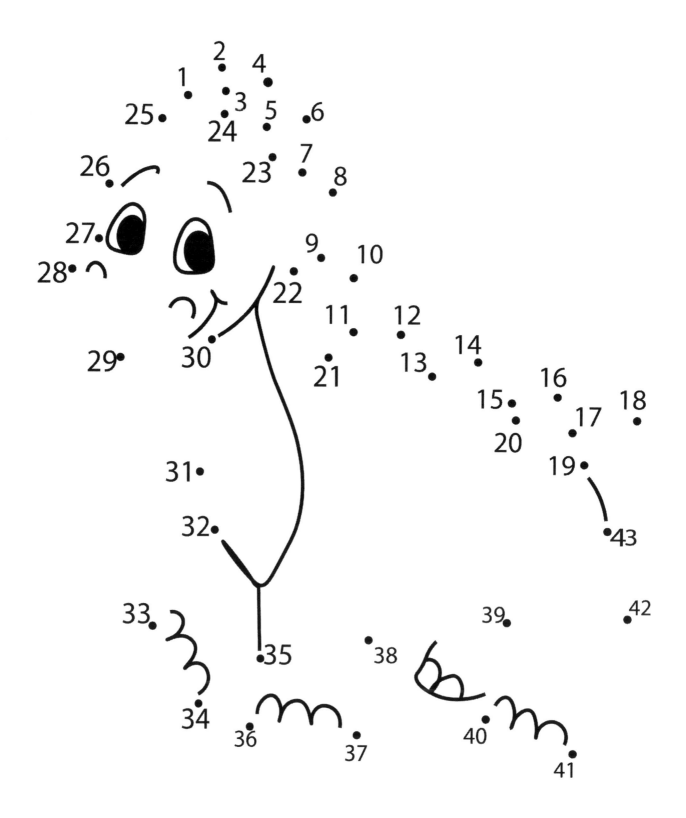

Level 3

Wow you made it far!

In this level, you will have to connect 20 + dots.

Ready? Let's go!

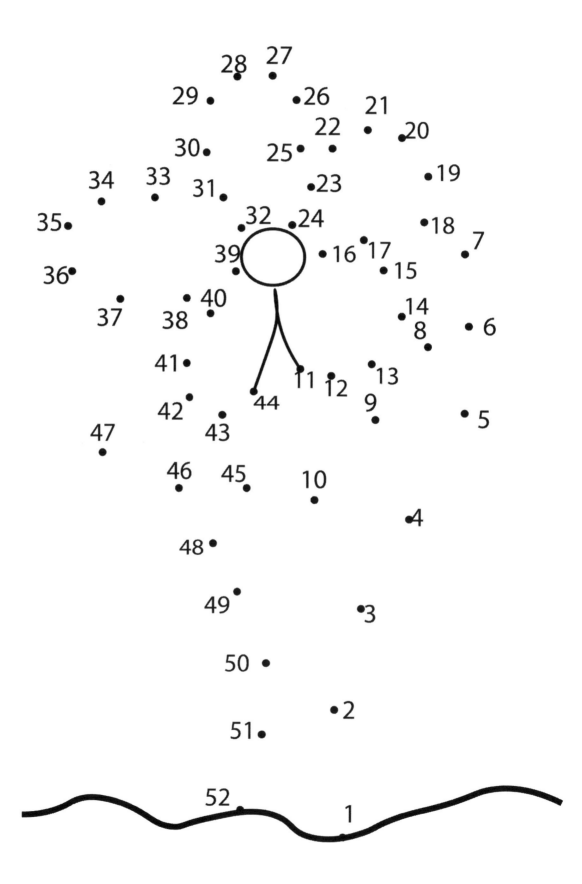

69

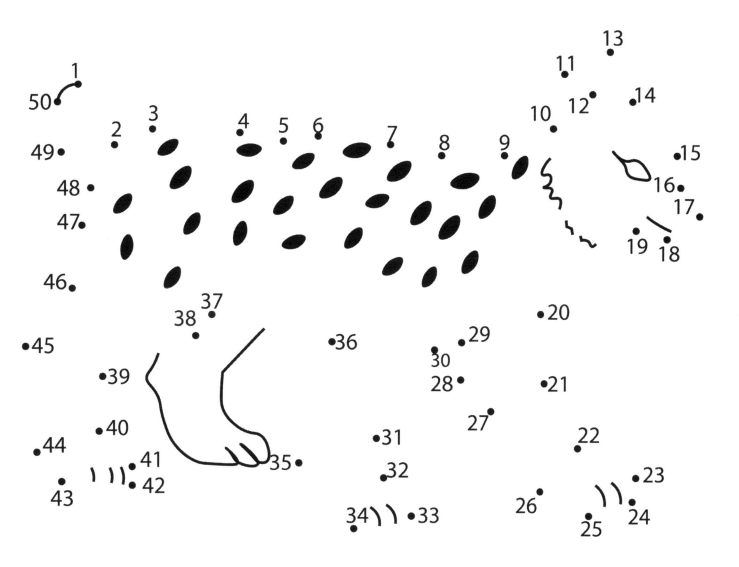

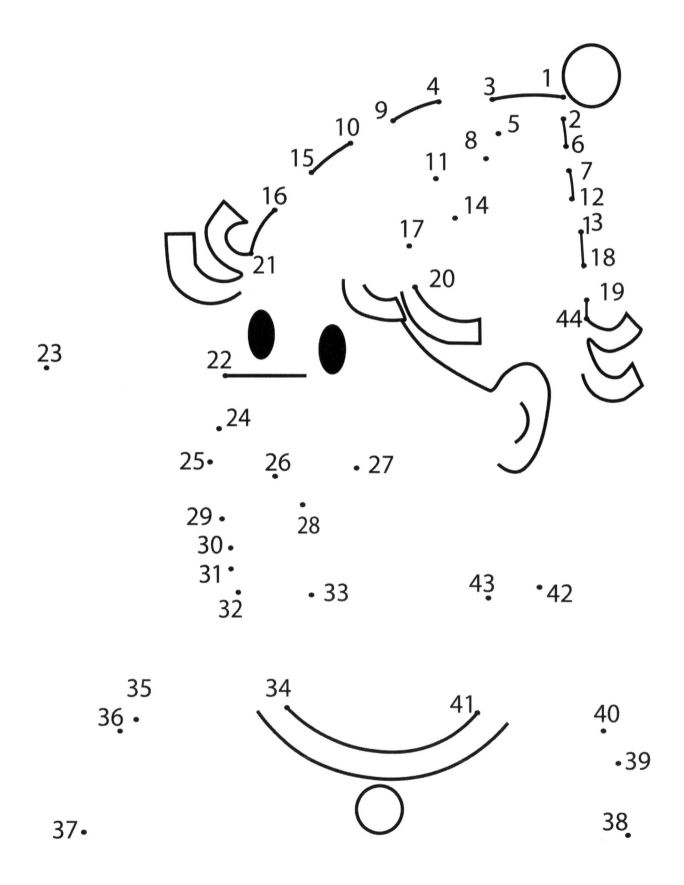

72

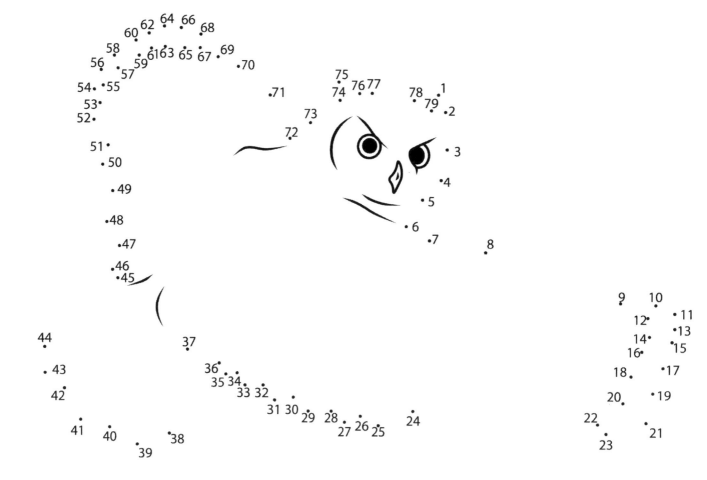

73

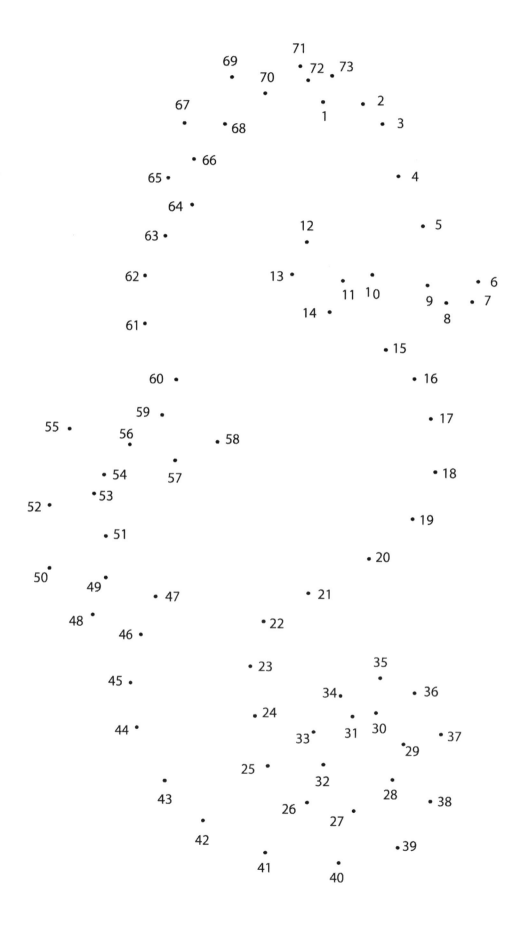

75

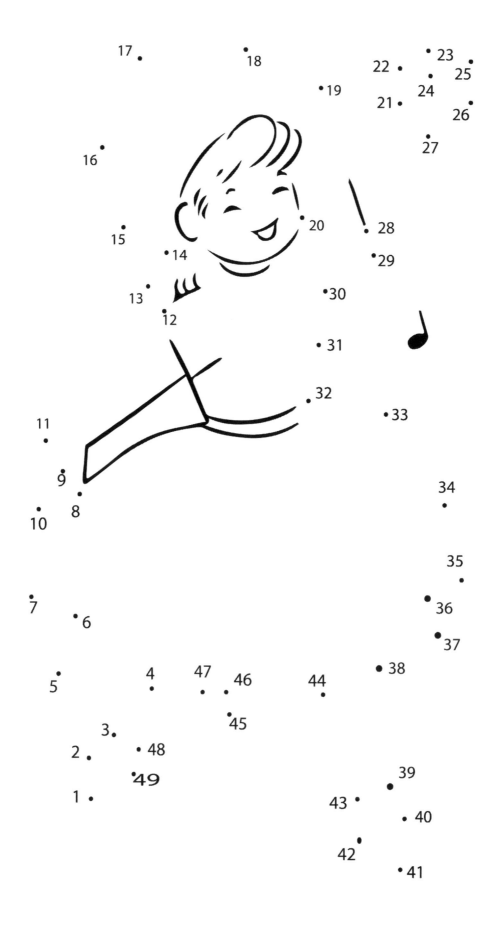

81

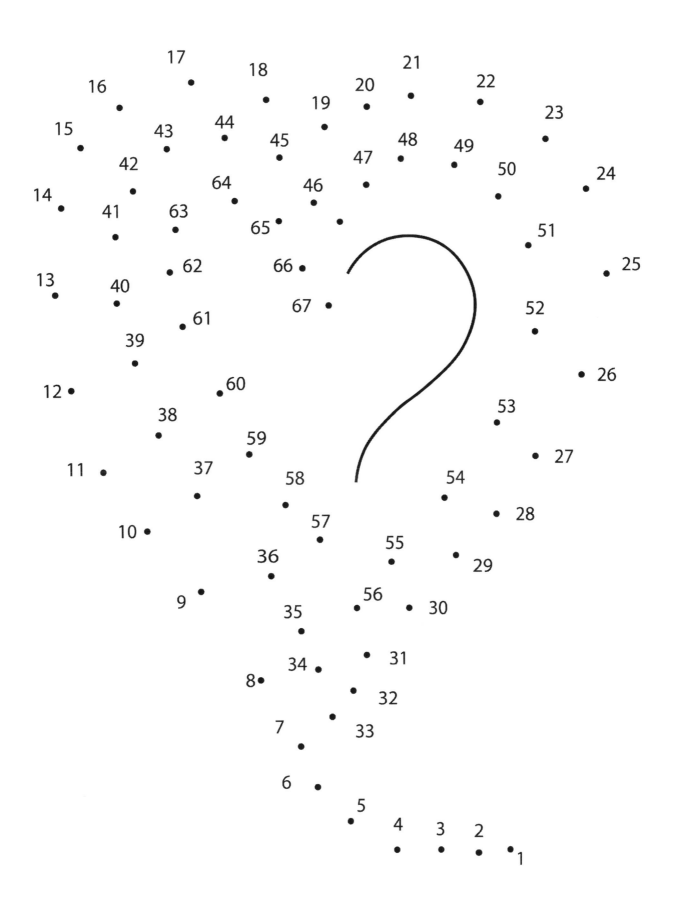

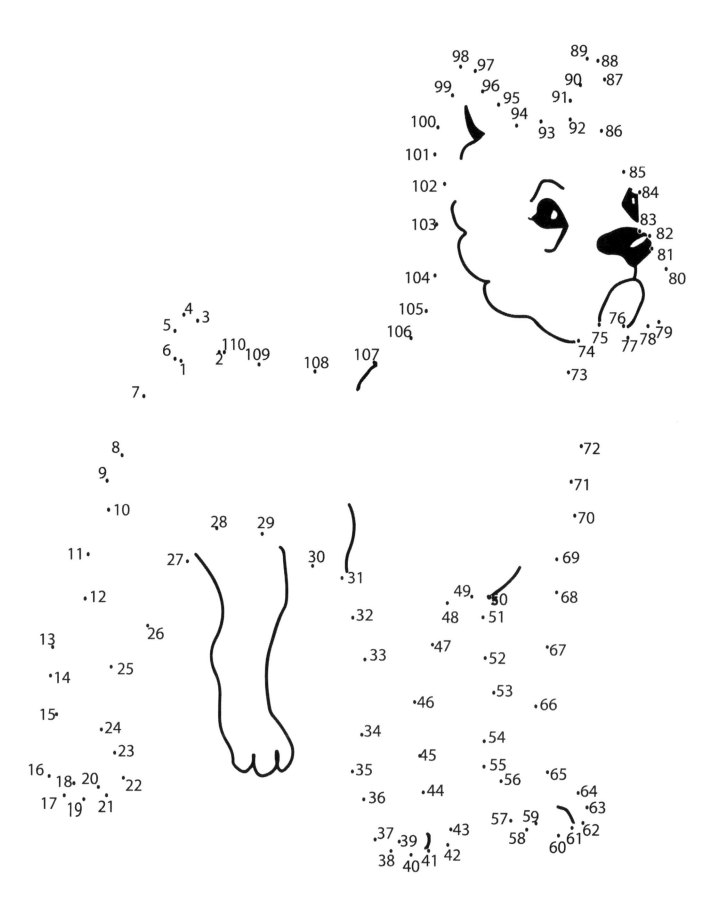

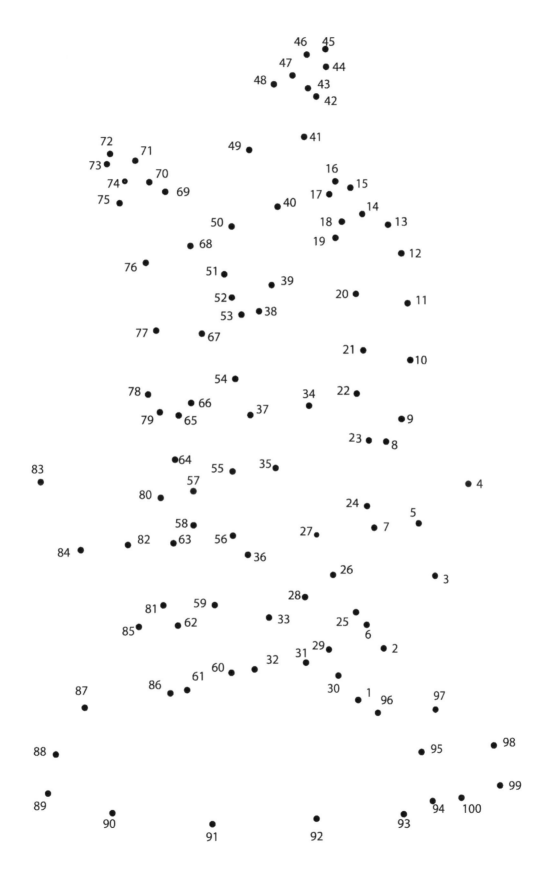

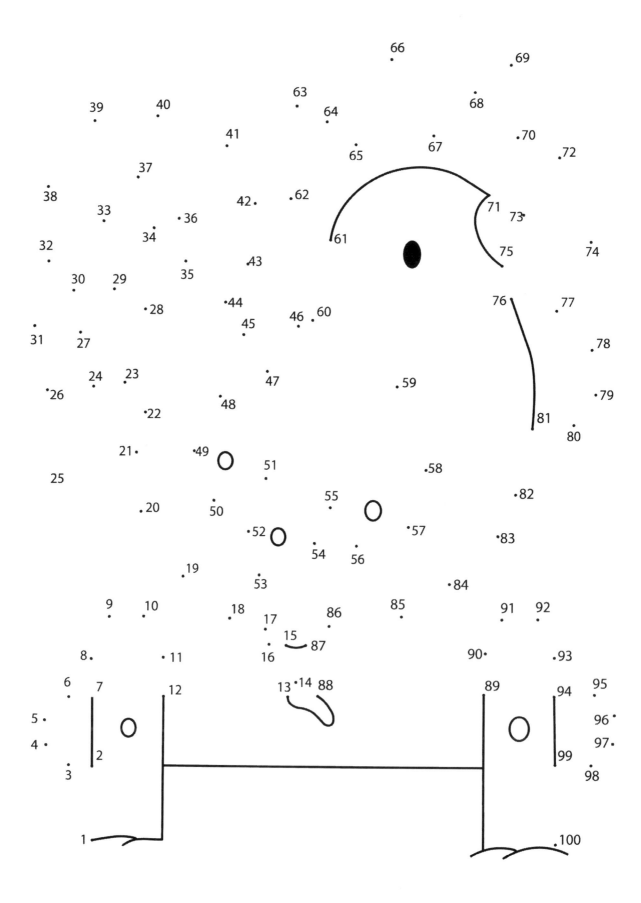

87

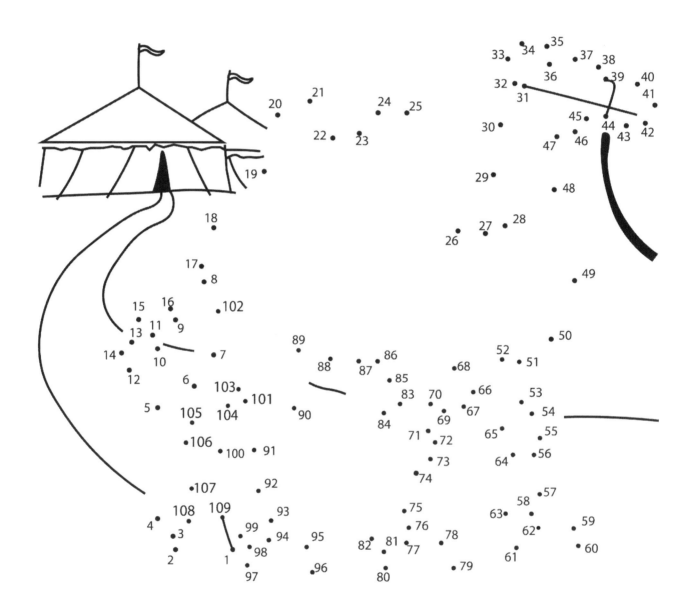

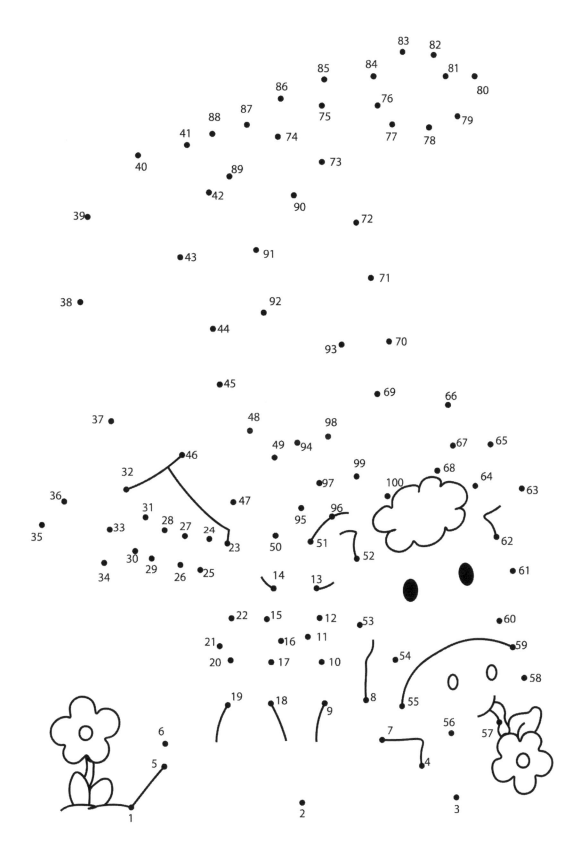

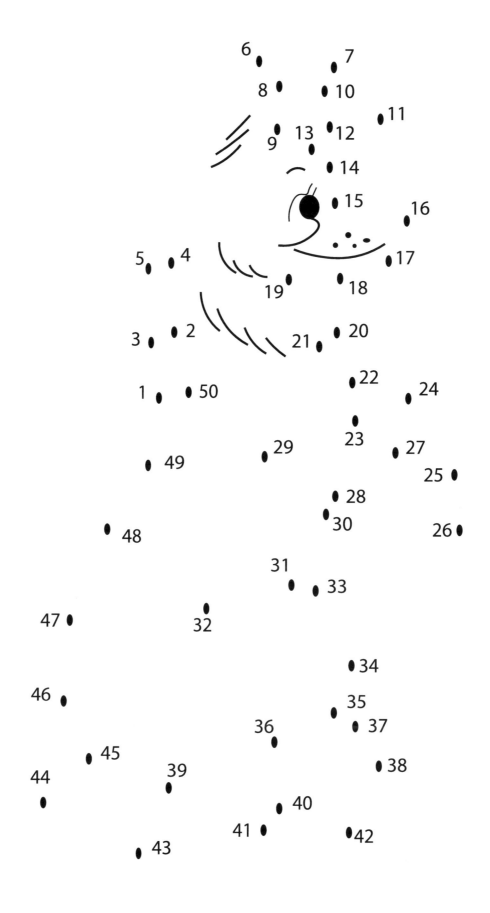

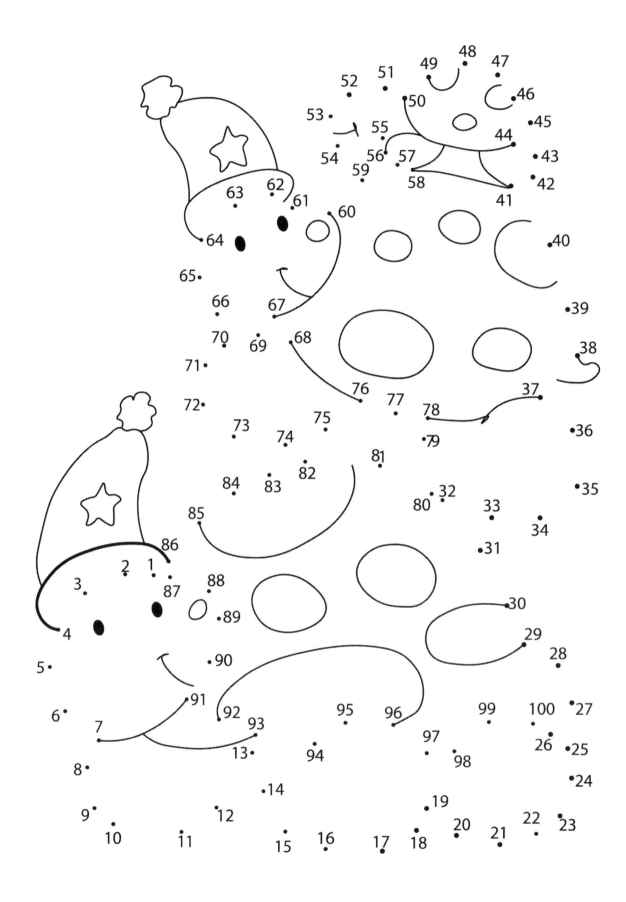

93

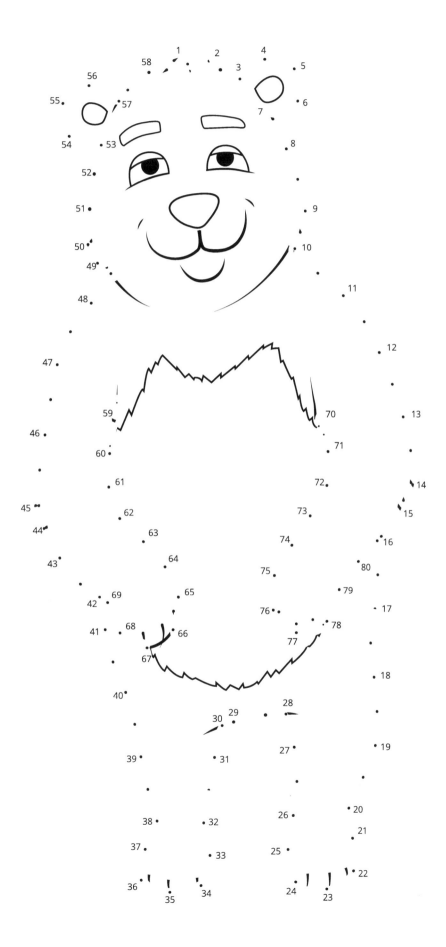

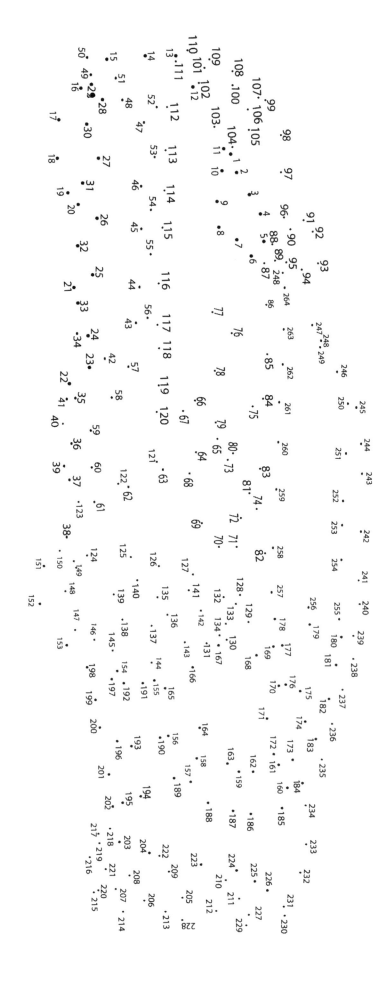

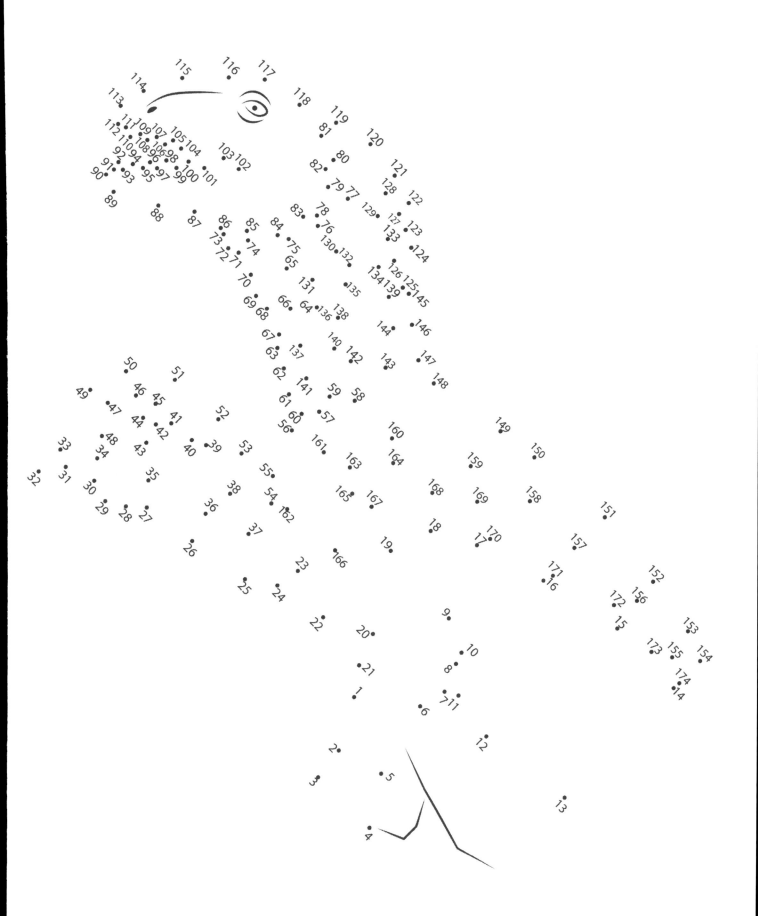

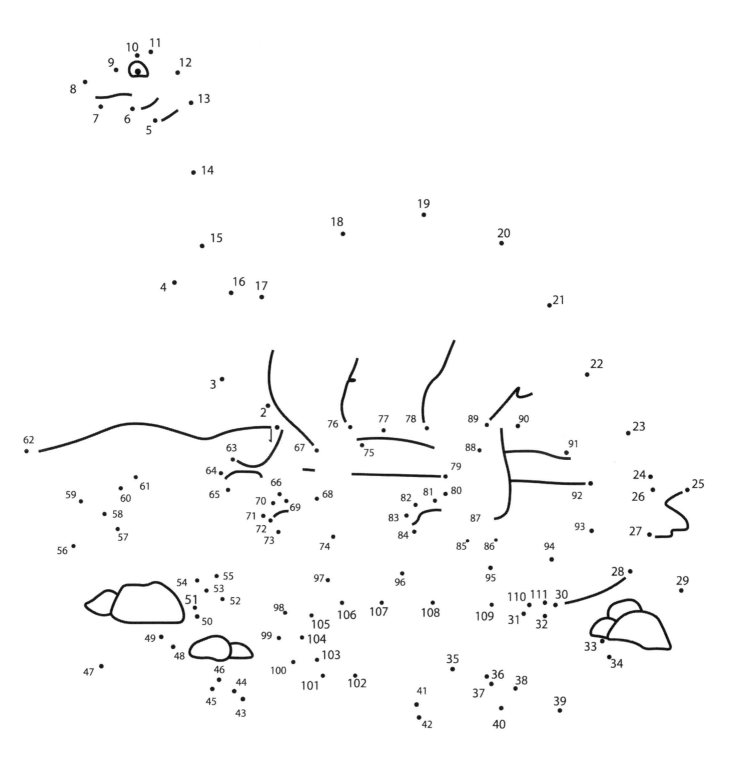

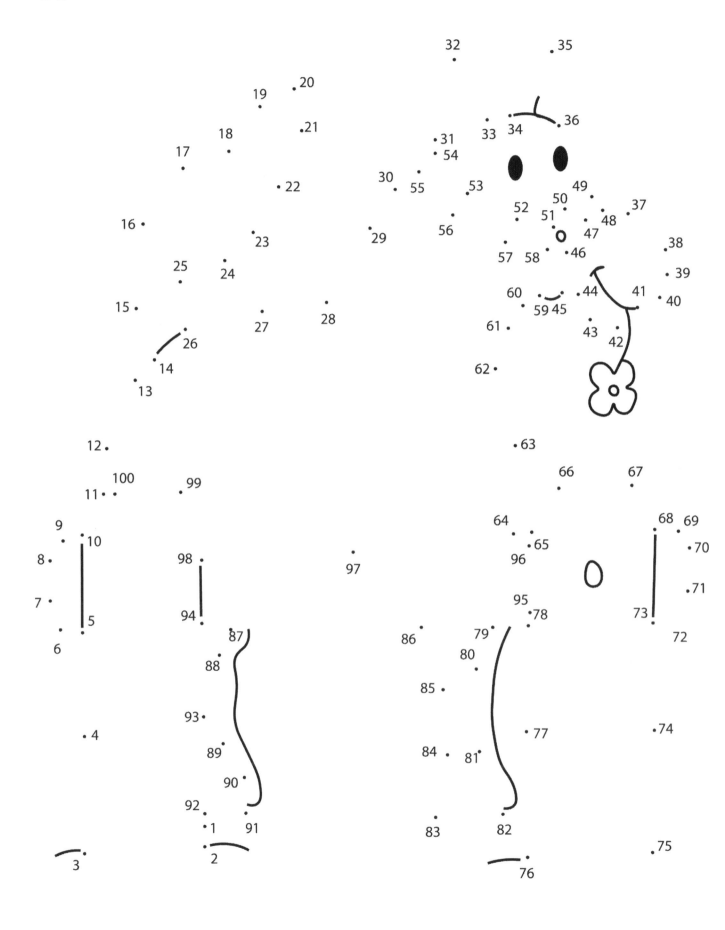

100

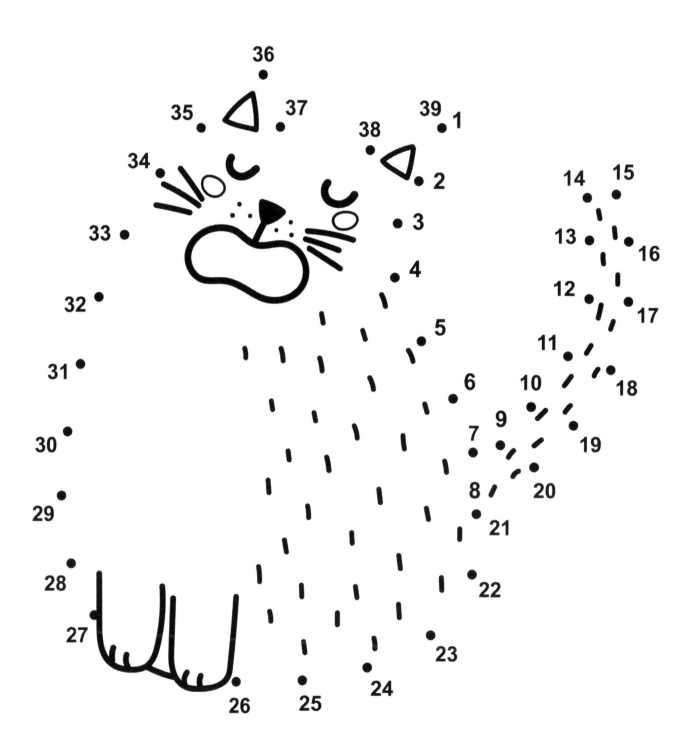

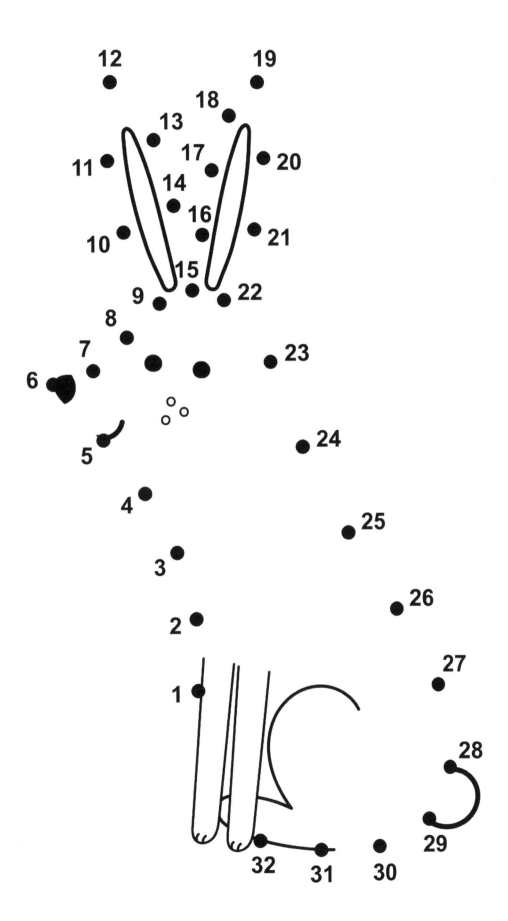

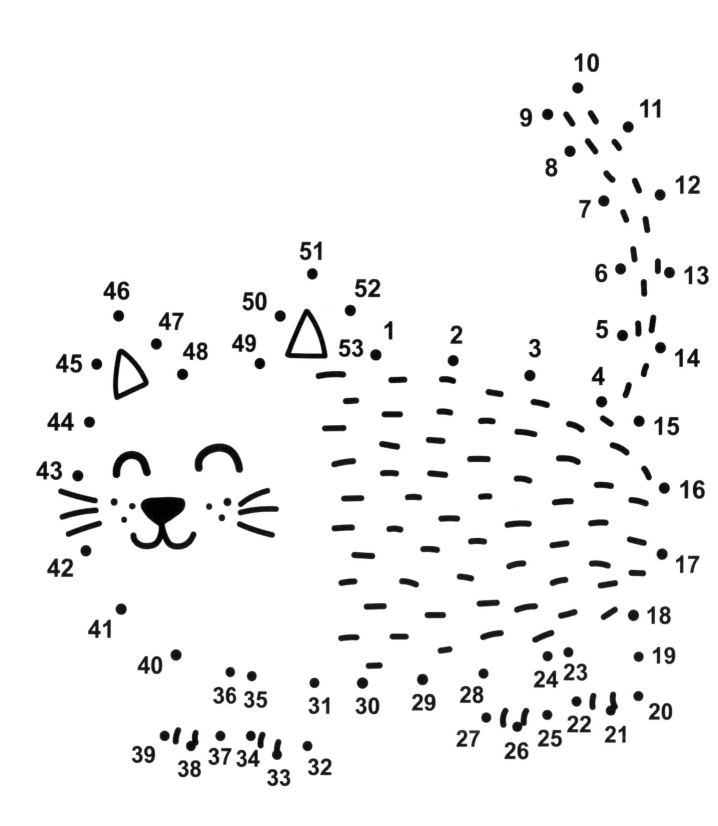

CONGRATULATIONS!

You're truly amazing! I am sure there are some obstacles along the way; it was great you persisted through and finished the job!

If you want to continue with more activities, just send me an email to support@kidsactivitybooks.org and I will send you some for free.

My name is Jennifer Trace and I hope you found this workbook helpful and fun. If you have any suggestions about how to improve this book, changes to make or how to make it more useful, please let me know.

If you like this book, would you be so kind and leave me a review on Amazon.

Thank you very much!
Jennifer Trace

Congratulations

Dot to Dot Star:

THE BEST!

_____

Date:_____   **Signed:**_____

Made in the USA
Middletown, DE
13 October 2021